MW01242221

PURSUING GOD

*Movements and Traditions
that Have Shaped Christianity
in The Western World*

*"God is spirit, and those who worship Him
must worship in Spirit and Truth."*
[The Lord Jesus, John 4:24]

by

Stacy W. Tyson

Pursuing God: Movements and Traditions
That Have Shaped Christianity in The Western World

Copyright © 2016
by Stacy W. Tyson and Truth Seekers Fellowship

ISBN-13: 978-1535076661
ISBN-10: 1535076666

For more information about Truth Seekers Fellowship:
www.tsfmemphis.org
email: connect@tsfmemphis.org

Contents

INTRODUCTION: A FRAME OF REFERENCE

"I pray not only for these, but also for those who believe in Me through their message. May they all be one, as You, Father, are in Me and I am in You. *May they also be one in Us, so the world may believe You sent Me*" (**The Lord Jesus**, John 17:19 *emphasis mine*).

In Ephesians 4:3, the Apostle Paul admonishes the church[1] to "make every effort to keep the unity/oneness of the Spirit in the bond of peace." The Holy Spirit has been given to Christ's people to bind them together as *one*, just as the Son is *one* with the Father.

In the longest recorded prayer of our Lord in John 17, Jesus ends with an appeal to the Father to knit His followers together as one so that, "the world may believe you sent me." Oneness—*the binding together of Christ's people in common thought and profession by love empowered by the Holy Spirit*—is THE most important evidence that He was sent from the Father to us. Where there is division among Christ's people, the reality of His mission is veiled.

This is a sobering way to start a book on the different factions and denominations and movements that have shaped Christianity. When we look at our history, we tend to see more failures than successes, more disasters than triumphs. However, *I am also completely convinced that in the sovereign and providential oversight of the Lord of the Church, He is working out plans and purposes that are clearly beyond our knowl-*

---

1   Throughout this work I have tried to consistently refer to the larger, universal, theological Church with a capital C. Where I reference the church in a local or denominational way I used the lower case c.

edge and comprehension so that His multifaceted wisdom will be displayed throughout the whole universe (See Ephesians 3:8-12).

With this being said, I believe it is of paramount importance for each and every follower of Jesus to understand not only *what* we believe, but also *why* we believe certain teachings and doctrines. We are going to outline the "what" and the "why" of many of the divisions and fractures have occurred within Christianity over the past 2000 years. Many of these splits were *necessary* as a response to a tradition that had strayed from The Truth of the Scriptures. Others were *not so necessary* and reflected the issue of *preference* rather than faithfulness to Christ.

How Do Our Thoughts Develop?

To understand how the various views that we will study have developed, it is important to understand the basic forces that have shaped these views. *We want to receive and communicate God's revelation with as few distortions as possible.* However, we must be aware that there are 'lenses' or biases that *shape* and sometimes *skew* the way we develop and practice theology. If we can understand the way these forces work, we will be better equipped to objectively evaluate not only the way we approach theology, but also be better equipped to analyze the way in which we view the world in general.

Understanding Where We Have Come from and Where We Are Heading

We all have to think about the World in which we live through our *experience*. Our experience is *always biased,* however, by powerful forces that work to shape our view of the world. The *three major forces* that affect the way we think about our world and ultimately impact our theology are represented in the following chart:

It is important to understand that these *influences* are always competing to pull our beliefs toward their gravitational center. They can each be *positive* or *negative* influences depending on how they are viewed and implemented into our worldview. The most powerful of these influences are **tradition** and **culture**. I would even argue that both *reason* and *experience* are really functions of these broader categories.

Tradition and culture are *vehicles* for information, knowledge, and wisdom. As we begin to think theologically and "do" theology, it is important to realize that good theology will always strive for a *balance* of these factors. Giving too much weight to any one will skew our view of the world, and ultimately our understanding of truth.

To understand these powerful forces, we must define them and take a brief look at their strengths and weaknesses. We will begin on the "inside" with our frame of reference—*our experience*—and then work our way out.

Experience

Experience can be defined as the sum total of all events that an individual has participated in or lived through which shapes his/her personality, attitudes, beliefs, etc. Everything we do is a process of our experience from driving a car to studying the Bible; experience is inescapable.

If we give a proper place to experience, our experience (properly evaluated!) *transforms knowledge into wisdom*. In this way, experience can bring balance to pure reason. However, we must be aware that experience can never establish THE Truth and that our experiences may be misunderstood. Your personal experience is too small to define *transcendent truth*.

At this point, it is important to state that this entire work assumes the existence and reality of *transcendent truth*. This is Truth, with a capital T, that exists above and beyond all traditional or cultural influences. In the West, until the time of the so-called Enlightenment, Transcendent Truth was thought to be synonymous with the Bible—the inspired and infallible Word of God given to us in human language. We are going to be working under the presupposition that, "God is there and He is not silent," to use Francis Schaeffer's phrase. Because there is a *transcendent* (He is above and beyond all other things) and *personal God* (He has made Himself know to us) there is a Truth that stands above time and space and ultimately beyond humanity's ability to manipulate. This transcendent God has revealed His reality in the communion of The Father, Jesus the Son, and the Holy Spirit.

Reason

Reason is the term I am using to refer to *the set of skills we use to think—to process information, ideas, and images*. It encompasses logic, rationality, analysis, and language. Used properly, reason guides us in proper thinking, and it provides a check and balance to our experience. However, we must also be aware of reason's weaknesses.

Our reason is inherently flawed by the fact that we cannot know all things that are necessary to know in order to comprehend certain topics fully and properly. And what is worse, our thinking about the world can simply be flawed because we are not thinking properly. *The greatest flaw in our thinking is thinking that we have no flaws in our thinking.*

Tradition

Tradition is a history of past events, decisions, beliefs that are shared in common within a certain group of people. Tradition is a powerful bias in terms of the way we view the world. It is a positive influence because the past helps us to understand the present. Tradition also provides balance to the force of culture which tends to focus on the "here and now." Tradition, however, may become too authoritative and crowd out all other alternatives. *Tradition wants to teach that the oldest answers are always right, but this is not always true.*

The Scriptures (The Bible)

Although The Scriptures are actually a part of Tradition, I am setting them apart as their own category. The Bible has been handed down to us and forms the foundation of every other Christian tradition. Not only have the Scriptures been handed down to us, the way we interpret them has been handed down as well.

By setting the Bible apart, I am again revealing a major tenet of my own worldview that I simply cannot set aside: The Scriptures hold a unique place in our common tradition as the Word of God, authoritative in and of themselves. As the Word of God, the Scriptures give us an infallible source of tradition and so extend as an arm of tradition that stands over all these other biases and influences. We know *what* the Scriptures say; the disagreement arises over what they *mean.*

Culture

Culture is the collective of behavior patterns, arts, beliefs, institutions, and all other products of human work and thought at *a given period in time among a specific people group (an "in crowd").* Culture can encompass something as large as a country or nation, or as small as a club of hobbyists or like-minded people.

It is important to remember that culture, in one sense, is a product of God's creation of humanity. We were created to exist in community. As such, the Bible shows that God communicated in and through culture, *not in spite of it.*

Culture, if interpreted properly, can bring balance to tradition as it realizes that history is moving forward and change is necessary. However, just as tradition, culture can become *too* authoritative in terms of defining what is accepted as "true." *Contrary to popular opinion, the newest answers are not always right.*

In time, *accepted culture becomes tradition.* Let me say that again because it is very important: *today's culture is producing the tradition of the future.*

Reason, experience and culture are topics which are touched upon throughout the length of these notes. *Tradition, however, is probably the main focus of this study.* In one sense, the various views of spirituality we are going to look at are all "traditions" in the broadest sense of the word.

As you begin to study these spiritual traditions it would be helpful for you to start to analyze them in terms of how they try to balance these four influences. Some will lean toward culture and experience, while others will rely heavily on tradition and reason as anchors for their belief and practice. Remember, a balanced view will recognize the strengths of each of these biases while at the same time trying to shore up the weaknesses.

The Incarnation of Ideas

In any work that is focused on the ideas and teachings of traditions, it is easy to get lost in the world of abstract, dehumanized ideas. Reading about the practices and beliefs of the Eastern Orthodox tradition is not the same as attending a service and hearing the sounds and smelling the smells. It is also not the same as getting to know someone who lives out the implications of the Eastern Orthodox faith.

Jesus took on human flesh to save us and in doing so He learned what it means to be human. These traditions have to be *experienced* in personal ways in order to really understand what they are about and to see that there is much openness and diversity of application among the many individuals who live *in* and live *out* these different "flavors" of Christian faith.

Traditions and Spirituality

We are going to be exploring these various movements and traditions on the "higher" level of theology and the pursuit of Truth. On the "lower" side, we need to consider how each of these affect the individual, day-to-day practice of the men and women who follow the diverse teachings of the various groups we will discuss. Simply put, the practical application of theological beliefs is what we call *spirituality*.

Being "spiritual" is back in fashion. Everyone from Hollywood celebrities to soccer moms agree that being a "spiritual person" is a virtue. Although there have been many books dealing with spirituality published in recent years, there is still quite a bit of ambiguity within Christian thought as to what "spirituality" means. T. R. Albin describes spirituality this way:

> "Christian spirituality involves the relationship between the whole person and a holy God, who reveals himself through both testaments—and supremely in the person of his unique Son, Jesus Christ. This relationship began at creation, but was broken by sin and can only be restored through faith in Jesus."

Although the language of "spirituality" is not prevalent in the New Testament there are insights which help us shape our understanding:

> "Now we have not received the spirit of the world, but the Spirit who comes from God, so that we may understand what has been freely given to us by God. We also speak these things, not in words taught by human wisdom, but in those taught by the Spirit, *explaining spiritual things to spiritual people*. But the unbeliever does not welcome what comes from God's Spirit, because it is foolishness to him; he is not able to understand it since it is evaluated spiritually. The spiritual person, however, can evaluate everything, yet he himself cannot be evaluated by anyone. For who has known the Lord's mind, that he may instruct Him? But we have the mind of Christ. (1 Corinthians 2:12–16 *emphasis mine*)

Here Paul describes a "spiritual person" as someone who has been enlightened and able to receive the knowledge of the Spirit of God

12

relating to Christ. A "spiritual person" in the Biblical sense is someone who is living under the guidance, direction, and enablement of The Holy Spirit. In a specifically Christian sense, *spirituality has to do with the Holy Spirit's interaction with the human spirit.*

It is important to realize that there are as many views of Christian spirituality as there are denominations and local churches. Particularly after the rise and influence of PostModernity and the emphasis on *individual experience,* Christianity has become a fragmented mosaic of spiritualities

In this book we are going to be exploring *some* of the major traditions and movements that have shaped and continue to guide the Christian understanding of spirituality and the pursuit of knowing and experiencing God more deeply.

From a holistic Biblical view, Spirituality is ultimately about *sanctification*—the process of being set apart and conformed to the likeness of Christ. Every tradition and movement that we will explore produces its unique view primarily in the way it links *justification* (being set right *with* God) to *sanctification* (being set apart and perfected *by* God).

As we shall see, even when we agree upon this goal not everyone takes the same path or comes to the same conclusions. It is important not only to see what these different conclusions are, but also to understand *why* and *how* they have developed.

Evaluating Our Beliefs

As much as is possible, I have tried to write *objectively*. I have resisted giving my own evaluation of the views that are discussed in hopes that you will be forced to think critically and analytically about the issues being presented. This book is really a collection of "research notes" in the sense that I have included many quotes from representatives of each of the views or scholars who have compiled works to help us understand each of the views better. Citations and references are included directly in the text marked off by parentheses () at the end of the sentence. The complete information for each reference can be found in the Bibliography.

Where criticisms or evaluations are made, these are a reflection of commonly accepted knowledge. However, in some cases I have been a little more "critical" when dealing with views that have shaped my beliefs. My goal is to stir up discussion and dialogue more than to tell you which view is *right* or which view is *wrong*.

Having said this, however, I must also say that it is my firm conviction that the Truth of Scripture provides the objective measure against which all views are to be evaluated. It is hard (impossible) for me to lay this basic belief aside. For this reason, I evaluate all teaching with two basic questions:

1. *Is this particular teaching (tradition, doctrine, etc.) based in Biblical Truth; Is it in-line with the revelation we have received?*

2. *Is this particular teaching (tradition, doctrine, etc.) focused toward Jesus Christ; Does it point us to Christ as The One above all things?*

These statements touch on the *major issue* that every tradition ultimately defines: *final authority. Who gets the final word on what is right and wrong, truth and lie, etc.?* As I just stated, I believe God has final authority in all things and He has communicated His authoritative Truth in the Scriptures. Many would agree with that statement. However, the dividing line is established in the question, "How is this final authority *delegated* through/to humanity?" This is the ultimate question that divides many of the major traditions we will discuss.

Studying the differing views of Christian Spirituality becomes a marvelous exercise in evaluating your own knowledge and comprehension of Scripture. In order to do an adequate job of evaluating these views, you must have some idea about how Scripture addresses each of the relevant issues. Again, I have not tried to tell you what Scripture has to say about any particular issue and to this end I have restrained, as much as possible, from giving you any of my own views so that you may see each tradition as clearly as possible.

To better understand the nature of different views of spirituality it is important to have an *objective format* in which to analyze the similarities and differences as well as strengths and weaknesses of each view.

Generally we may evaluate theses different traditions using four basic questions with some sub-questions for analysis and comparison:

Question 01: What is the basis for authority in the system?

- Objective: How does the system view Scripture and/or Tradition and what weight does it give to each?
- Subjective: How does the system deal with religious experience?

Question 02: What role does the believer play in the process of spiritual growth?

- Integration: Can the view be lived out? Does it make sense in light of common Christian experience?

Question 03: What is the role of the local assembly (local church) in the process of spiritual growth?

- What authority does the church have over the life of the believer?
- How do the Ordinances (Holy Sacraments) contribute to one's spirituality?
- What responsibility does the believer have in the functioning of the local church?
- What responsibility does the Community of Believers (The Church) have to society and culture?

Question 04: How does the view evaluate or quantify spiritual growth?

- Can spiritual growth be measured?
- Should Spiritual growth be measured?
- If so, how?

When thinking about and studying the various approaches to spirituality it is helpful to think around these basic questions. In doing so, what the views share in common as well as how they differ will be made apparent. These questions may also be used to clarify the way the different traditions handle the passages of Scripture which speak to these issues.

With this in mind, we must also note that there are four general tendencies or influences which occur in all representative Christian movements or groups:

1. **Traditionalists** (Conservatives)—This group submits to the authority of the tradition and try to live in obedience to the teachings of the tradition.

2. **Culturals**—These people are associated to a particular tradition by birth, they have a loose association with the local church but do not generally submit to its teachings

3. **Liberals**—These defy the traditional institution by calling into question its major historical and biblical doctrines.

4. **Charismatics**—This group places great emphasis on personal experience to determine the content of faith and piety.

These groups are present in all Christian denominations and sects. There are liberal Baptists and there are cultural Baptists. There are charismatic cultural Roman Catholics. These categories are not defined so we can measure a person up, but instead to understand where they have come from and where they are headed.

A Word About Diversity and Our Uniqueness

In discussing the various views, it becomes impossible not to over generalize when speaking about any tradition. However, it must be kept in mind that these traditions and views are not *monolithic*. Within each view, there is a great fabric of diversity that can only be explored by your personal, continued study. There are liberal Catholics as well as Protestants. There is even such a thing as Calvinistic Methodists! My goal here is not to say that if you are a Methodist or if you are Reformed you believe and practice everything we discuss about that particular tradition. Instead, I wish only to *highlight the key doctrines and movements that have provided the foundation for the expression of each of these traditions and the core beliefs that have shaped the general trajectory of the tradition.*

As individuals, we each probably have more of an *eclectic spirituality.* We have all been influenced by many traditions, authorities, and views that have shaped our particular and unique pursuit of God. While researching, I read articles written by an Eastern Orthodox theologian who sees the need for a greater evangelical emphasis and Bible literacy in his tradition and calls for this change. I also encountered an Evangelical Baptist who received spiritual counsel and direction from a Roman Catholic. *Father-God is writing a unique story with each of our lives that displays some facet of His grace and wisdom in a unique way.*

Having said that, I must also say that *I do not believe that all of the teachings and ideas that will be presented here are in line with The Truth and a Biblical, Christ-focused worldview.* The goal of this work is to simply expose you to some of the movements and traditions that have got us to where we are today.

Keeping the Goal in Sight

We began talking about the "oneness/unity of the Spirit." In Ephesians 2, Paul makes the case that the blood of Christ brings reconciliation to the Jews and Gentiles, people groups once separated by theological and ethnic division. This peace comes *in* and *through* Jesus *by* the Spirit:

> "But now in Christ Jesus, you who were far away have been brought near by the blood of the Messiah… For through Him we both have access by one Spirit to the Father." (Ephesians 2:13-18)

In the context of Ephesians 4, one of the effects of the Holy Spirit's work among Christ's people is to bind them together as one in common confession of fundamental Christian belief:

> "There is one body and one Spirit—just as you were called to one hope at your calling—4:5 one Lord, one faith, one baptism, 4:6

one God and Father of all, who is above all and through all and in all. (Ephesians 4:4–6)

For this reason, Paul instructs the Ephesians to "be eager to maintain this unity/oneness that the Spirit produces." The Holy Spirit of God is the Spirit of reconciliation and peace, binding Christ's people together in love.

For every true Christian, every true follower of Christ, there should be one focus and goal for life: *Jesus Christ*. Because He is Truth and the Truth is found in Him, we need to know Him deeply and personally. If we are truly following Him and seeking Him, we are being transformed into His image, conformed to His likeness. The Holy Spirit has been given to us to give us communion with the Father and the Son and also to empower us for life. We also need help from other mature Christ-followers; *we cannot do it alone*. So as we begin, we should do so in humility, remembering the wisdom attributed to Rupertus Meldenius:

> *"In necessary things, unity;*
> *in doubtful things, liberty;*
> *in all things, charity."*

Hopefully by understanding where we have come from, we can gain a better understanding of where we are and move forward in grace and truth, captivated by the glorious vision of "all things being summed up in Christ" and reconciled in Him (Ephesians 1:7-10, Colossians 1:19-20). Despite all the doctrines that divide us now, in the end Christ will have His way and we will all,

> "…live as one with one another, according to the command of Christ Jesus, so that we may glorify the God and Father of our Lord Jesus Christ with a united mind and voice."
> (Romans 15:5–6 *translation mine*)

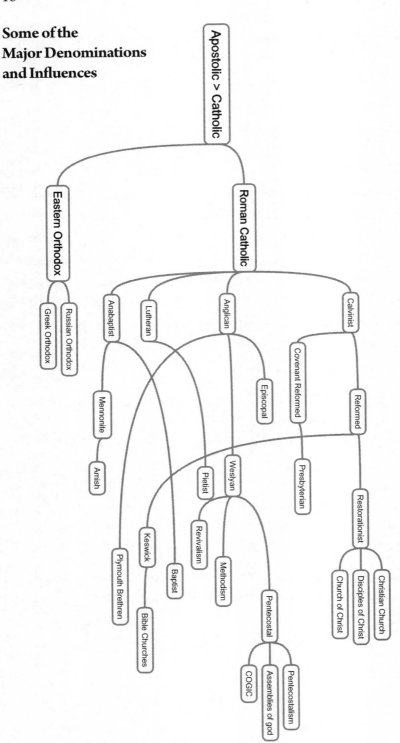

18

Some of the Major Denominations and Influences

MOVEMENTS IN THE ANCIENT WORLD

The oldest expression of Christianity is found in the churches established by the work of the Apostles in the First Century. However, the record of their theology and practice is found primarily in the letters of the New Testament.[2] Since most Christian traditions and denominations claim at least to be following the principles the First Century Church, we will not begin with an examination of this first church. *Instead we will survey the history of how Christianity has been fragmented over the issue of what these original documents mean in terms of life and godliness.*

The two oldest expressions of Christian spirituality past the First Century are preserved in the Roman Catholic and Eastern Orthodox traditions. Though there are several major differences in the doctrine of these traditions, they are nevertheless related by a common origin and a common set of controversies.

From around AD 100 to 300 early Christianity developed in the midst of persecution from the Roman Empire. During this period many of the central doctrines of Christianity were formulated. Issues of **orthodoxy** (what one must believe to be a Christian) and **heresy** (teaching which is clearly contrary to the truth of Scripture) were

---

2 Since these letters are "occasional" (written to address specific circumstances) they do not give us much information about the actual "practice" of these early believers in everyday life. In the NT we do not find a simple "blueprint for the perfect church." This is not to say that the NT is ambiguous about what is pleasing to God. The principles that for Godly living have been clearly set forth in the Bible, its just that most don't take the time or effort to do the hard work of discovering this truth and applying it to life.

hammered out in the writings of the early **Apostolic Fathers.** These Fathers were the Bishops and leaders who knew the Apostles and exerted great influence over the Church.

From AD 200—300 the **Apologists** and their works took root in the growing Christian movement. From its very beginning, Christianity stood at odds with the Roman Empire. Until the Edict of Toleration in AD 313, Roman policies escalated the persecution of Christians as an "illegal" religion. The Apologists were the theologians who gave *reasonable defenses* to the questions of why anyone would be a Christian.

Although for the first three centuries, there were several factions within Christianity, persecution prevented these various groups from organizing and consolidating their teaching and practices into alternative forms of the Christian faith. *All this changed with Constantine.*

Both the Roman Catholic and Eastern Orthodox tradition were united in the *Old Catholic Church* which is the title given to Christianity from the First Century, through Constantine's edict of Toleration in AD 313 and on into the 4th and 5th Centuries.[3] Christianity was referred to as the *catholic* Church during this time meaning that there was *only one* true Christianity and Church. Later, the term catholic became uniquely linked to the Roman Catholic church.

The ancient Church, just as the Roman empire, was split both *geographically* and *theologically* by East and West. The West was largely influenced by the theology and writings of the Latin Church Fathers (Clement of Rome, Hermas, etc.), whereas the East developed under the Greek Fathers (Ignatius, Polycarp, Papias, etc.).

The **Seven Ecumenical Councils** are central to the development of Christianity in this era as they defined the Church's view on the nature of Christ, specifically the relationship between His human and divine

---

3   This edict (The Edict of Milan) recognized Christianity as a valid religion
     and thus ended the long and vicious persecution of Christianity by Roman
     Imperialism. The actual persecution was ended by the Edict of Galerius in
     311. Constantine—the first "Christian Emperor"— is given credit for the
     beginning of this "golden age" for early Christianity.

The Seven Ecumenical Councils

AD 325 Nicea 1

This is the foundational church council whose formulations have been accepted and affirmed by all orthodox forms of Christianity. It established the relationship between God the Father and God the Son (Jesus) thus clearly affirming the deity of Jesus. It refuted **Arianism** which denied Christ's deity. The deity of Christ was stated in the Nicaean Creed which also clearly communicated the *trinitarian* nature of orthodox belief.

AD 381 Constantinople 1

Fortified the conclusions of Nicea and also refuted the teachings of **Apollonarianism** which taught that Jesus had a human body, but that his mind and soul were divine, not human.

AD 431 Ephesus

Refuted **Nestorianism** which taught that Jesus was two persons - one divine, one human. This entailed the growing controversy of calling Mary "the mother of God" which Nestorius opposed. This council affirmed the basis for the *hypostatic union*—Jesus was one person with two natures, neither mixed nor mingled.

AD 451 Chalcedon

Refuted the teachings of **Eutychian Monophysitism** which claimed that Jesus had only one nature, *fused together* in one person.

AD 553 Constantinople 2

Met to deal with the growing rift between the Nestorian and Monophysite factions of the Church.

AD 681 Constantinople 3

Refuted **Monotheletism** which taught that Jesus had two natures but *one will*.

AD 787 Nicaea 2

Refuted the Synod of Hieria (753), convened by Emperor Constantine V, which declared that images of Jesus, Mary, and the Saints were idolatrous—*the iconoclastic controversy.*

"natures." These seven councils are called *ecumenical* because they were generally attended by bishops and leaders from all throughout the empire, both East and West, although there are a few exceptions. In the final analysis, these Councils affirmed that in order for Christ to be the Eternal Savior He had to be both God *and* Man—The God-Man. (See "The Seven Ecumenical Councils" on page 21 for a basic overview of these councils.)

In hammering out the issues of orthodoxy, the councils would often produce a creed that gave a summary of the key beliefs that defined their conclusions. One creed, the *Nicene Creed*, is a prominent example of the systematizing work that was done in this era:

> We believe in one God, the Father, the Almighty,
> maker of heaven and earth, of all that is,
>> both seen and unseen.
> We believe in one Lord, Jesus Christ, the only Son of God
>> eternally begotten of the Father, God from God,
> Light from Light, true God from true God,
>> begotten, not made, one in Being with the Father.
> Through him all things were made.
> For us men and for our salvation
>> he came down from heaven.
> By the power of the Holy Spirit he was born
>> of the Virgin Mary, and became man.
> For our sake he was crucified under Pontius Pilate;
>> he suffered, died, and was buried.
> On the third day he rose again
>> in fulfillment of the Scriptures;
> He ascended into heaven
>> and is seated at the right hand of the Father.
> He will come again in glory
>> to judge the living and the dead,
>> and His kingdom will have no end.
> We believe in the Holy Spirit,
>> the Lord, the giver of life,

who proceeds from the Father and the Son.
With the Father and Son He is worshiped and glorified.
He has spoken through the prophets.
We believe in one holy catholic and apostolic Church.
We acknowledge one baptism for the forgiveness of sins.
We look for the resurrection of the dead,
and the life of the world to come.

The Great Schism of 1054

By the 7th Century with Pope Gregory I, the differences in *western* and *eastern* theological emphasis and exposition were widening. This division reached critical mass in the 11th Century resulting in the *Great Schism of 1054*. This event marks the clear distinguishing of the Eastern Orthodox (old eastern church) and the Roman Catholic (old western church) traditions.

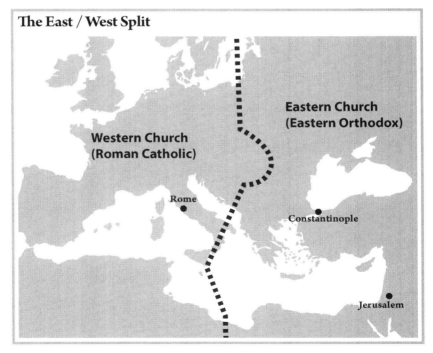

Although the causes of the The Schism were many, two major theological issues precipitated the split: the use of icons in worship and the line in the *Nicene Creed* which states that the Holy Spirit proceeds from the Father *and* the Son, the so called *filioque* controversy.[4] The Eastern church argued that icons, graphic depictions of Christ or the Saints, were to be used as symbols both of reverence and instruction in the life of the believer. John of Damascus said, "What the Scripture is to those who can read, the icon is to the illiterate" (Cunliffe-Jones 197). Although this practice was not denounced entirely by the Western church, it nevertheless became a divisive element and distinguishing mark of the Eastern church. Disagreement on this issue led to the *iconoclastic controversies* in which one group called for the destruction of all icons and images as idolatrous.

The *Nicene Creed* controversy, however, was the final blow in the controversies which divided East and West. The phrase *"from the Son"* in the Nicene Creed in reference to the *procession* of the Holy Spirit was included by Western fathers who asserted that the Holy Spirit proceeds from the Father *and* the Son. The Eastern fathers, primarily Photius of Constantinople, rejected this idea based on John 15:26 and affirmed that the Spirit proceeds only from the Father. Unable to come to any form of agreement, the two factions split over this detail of theology.

As I said, it is beyond the scope of our purposes here to explore all of the subtle but significant theological differences that caused the split of the Western and Eastern church in 1054. It is a truly complex issue on a theological level *but easier to understand on a worldly level.* The Schism essentially came down to a "fist-fight" over who is at the top of the earthly hierarchy of *authority.*

By the time we get to the 11th Century, the Church exerted not only great spiritual power but also great political and cultural power. When Constantine moved the capital of the Roman Empire from Rome to ancient Byzantium (renamed *Constantinople,* modern day *Istanbul*) a rift was cut that would ultimately lead to the fracture of 1054.

---

4   *filioque* (Latin for "from the Son"). There were many other controversies involved: Papal succession through Peter, celibacy of the priesthood, use of unleavened bread in the Eucharist, etc. However, these two were key.

Now, there would be a fight over who had final earthly authority in the Church: the Bishop of Rome (The Pope) or the Patriarch of Constantinople. In 1053 the Patriarch of Constantinople ordered the closure of all Western-Latin churches in the city in response to the Pope's command for the Eastern-Greek churches in southern Italy to conform to Latin practices or close. In 1054 Pope Leo IX sent a delegation to Constantinople to challenge Patriarch Michael I Cerularius' claim to be "Ecumenical Patriarch" (essentially meaning head over all the churches, including Rome) and reasserting The Pope's claims of final earthly authority. The episode ended with both sides *excommunicating* the other. The divide exists to this day.

After the Schism, the distinctive theology of the two traditions developed largely by the differing philosophical assumptions of the major theologians in each line. Beginning in the 12th and 13th centuries, there was a move to integrate classic Greek philosophy with Christian theology particularly in the Western Roman Catholic church. The Roman Catholic tradition was largely shaped by *a return to Aristotelian logic* in the works of Thomas Aquinas and his successors. In Aristotle's teaching *man can perceive truth in nature and can reason to absolutes.* Truth can be attained solely by reason (induction and deduction). Man can see facts in nature and reason to absolute conclusions about God and existence. This method lays the foundation for the flowering of logic and reason in pre-Enlightenment Europe. This strand of theology relied heavily on a new application of scholastic discipline in which philosophy became the new tool of shaping theology.

The Eastern Orthodox tradition, however, developed it's theology more in line with a *Neoplatonic* approach which is skeptical of our ability to arrive at truth through our perceptions of nature. Our ability to truly perceive is flawed. To attain ultimate truth, one must not be blinded by the illusions of this world, but through the experience of the transcendent see through to the reality that is beyond. This led to a more *speculative approach* to the development of doctrine.[5] God is a

---

5   Whereas Aristotle's philosophy is rooted in nature, Platonism and

being of personal beauty, to be worshiped in awe, not merely an object to be studied or "figured out."

Understanding how these two ancient traditions developed is foundational for understanding the many diverse traditions present in Christianity today. Ultimately, the Roman Catholic line of tradition would divide again in the 16th Century during The Great Reformation. This divide would produce Protestantism and the thousands of denominations that would spring up afterwards. The Eastern Orthodox Church has never experienced any split or transformation like the Great Reformation and so exists as the oldest, unbroken tradition within Christianity.

NeoPlatonism places greatest emphasis on the world of "forms"—abstractions that define yet transcend experience. Experience in nature and reality can only produce fallible opinions. Truth is found absolutely only in the world of "forms." The 'forms' are spiritual—pure representations of what we see in reality.

Roman Catholicism

As we begin to explore these traditions and movements, the first thing to decide is where to start. The two oldest traditions of the Christian faith are the Roman Catholic and Eastern Orthodox. We could start with either and a good case could be made to begin with Easter Orthodoxy as it preserves the oldest liturgy and probably the closest connection (in a certain sense) with the most ancient Apostolic Fathers.

We are going to begin, however, with Roman Catholicism. I begin here because I am assuming that most of my readers are more influenced by the Western tradition of early Christianity and will have more in common with this view. Understanding the foundation laid in Roman Catholicism gives us a framework to build on in terms of similarities and differences with all the other traditions.

The Authority of the Pope (Apostolic Succession)

To understand the foundation of Roman Catholic spirituality, we have to begin with the doctrine of Apostolic Succession. This is the teaching that the Pope (The Bishop of Rome) receives his authority from Peter (The first Apostolic Bishop of Rome) through an unbroken line of subsequent bishops. In other words, The Pope is seen as the historical successor to Peter and the representative and spokesman for Christ on earth.

Why is this such a key issue? Roman Catholic theologians argue that Jesus delegated authority to Peter and gave him the keys to the Kingdom (see Matthew 16:18-19) and thus final human authority to represent Christ on Earth. Peter is also seen as the "rock" upon which the Church is built. It is argued that Peter was the first bishop of Rome and therefore all subsequent bishops of Rome receive the authority of Peter through the laying on of hands and other formal rites.

The Pope is viewed as the Vicar of Christ, that is, the representative of Christ on the earth. As the power of the Papacy developed, the doctrine of the infallibility of the Pope also took solid form. This doctrine teaches that The Pope has the ability and authority to speak *ex cathedra* which makes his words authoritative for the entire Church.[6] This essentially gives him authority *equal* to that of Scripture. Interestingly, this right has been invoked rarely in the history of the Roman Catholic church.

However, the Pope's authority worked out in the various councils and proclamations of the Roman Catholic church has shaped the form of this tradition. The Pope coupled with the hierarchy (Cardinals, Bishops, etc.) and the Priesthood play an authoritative and mediatorial role in the life of the believer.

The Mediatorial Role of the Priesthood

For the Roman Catholic, *God's grace is mediated through the priesthood of the church.* The Faith and it's practice are not matters left to the subjectivity of the individual, but are regulated by the edict of the institutional church with the Pope being the final human authority. The institution of the church is the locus of authority for the Roman Catholic. As such, tradition plays a great role both in Catholic theology and spirituality.

Roman Catholic doctrine draws heavily on the writings of the early Fathers who also emphasized the role of the Bishops and Priests:

> "As the Lord was united to the Father and did nothing without him… so neither should you do anything without the bishop and priests" (Ignatius quoted by Hahn 81).

To be clear on these points, we must understand that by the time these doctrines solidified into their present forms, many things had "evolved" out of the views of the ancient Church. The Apostolic Fathers viewed THE Church more in terms of the people who were bound together in Christ through the work of the Holy Spirit. By the middle ages The Roman Catholic church understood itself more in terms of

---

6   The First Vatican council (1870) under Pope Pius IX stated that a Pope spoke *ex cathedra* by his claim to be "pastor and teacher of all Christians," and therefore, "he defined a doctrine concerning faith and morals to be held by the universal Church."

the *institution*. It had become a vast religious and political reality, deeply rooted in *the tradition* that most shaped Western culture.

The institutional church became viewed a the "mother church"— the physical representation on Earth of the Father-Son-Spirit-Saints family in Heaven. Cyprian famously said, "He can no longer have God for his father, who has not the Church for his mother."

The Sacramental System

Thomas Aquinas is generally thought of as the great theologian of Roman Catholicism. Although he writes in the 13th Century after many centuries of turmoil and expansion within the Roman church, his theology is the backbone of Roman Catholic spirituality as it is practiced today. His theology shapes the Roman Catholic view of The Sacraments.

The Holy Sacraments are the means by which one *grows in the grace and favor of God*. These Sacraments are based in Aquinas' formulation of *merit* and *co-operative grace*. Before meriting anything, one must make retribution for sin and be reconciled to God. Aquinas called this the First Grace accomplished through Christ. From this First Grace the Christian becomes capable of *doing other meritorious works* thereby increasing grace and the ability to do good works to merit more grace and the ability to do more good. "Aquinas view of the spiritual life can best be expressed as a spectrum ranging from sinfulness to perfection. This understanding of Aquinas helps define the accomplishments of each sacrament" (Burge "Sin, Mortal").

As already stated, The Sacraments become the key means in the church through which grace is given. The seven sacraments are:

1. **Baptism**: washes away original sin of infants, not applied to adults

2. **Holy Eucharist**: the *actual* Body and Blood of Jesus present in the bread and wine (transubstantiation); to be partaken of each week as spiritual sustenance

3. **Confirmation:** membership in the church is confirmed after a child is taught the doctrines of the church (The Catechism)

4. **Penance**: sins are absolved by confession to a priest usually accompanied by a prescribed action to show remorse for sin

5. **Matrimony**: union of man and woman by the blessing of the priest

6. **Holy Orders**: Monasticism, men enter priesthood or teach, women join convents or do social work, seen as total devotion to God

7. **Extreme Unction/Anointing of the sick**: the offering of communion by a priest to the dying to make sure the soul is prepared for eternity. In recent times this has been expanded to include the anointing of the sick.

For the Roman Catholic, life moves from a state of sinfulness to a state of perfection affected by the application of grace through The Sacraments. Most Catholics take part in six of The Sacraments with Holy Orders being reserved for priests and nuns only.

The application of grace though The Sacraments cannot offset *mortal sin* which are sins the church has defined as causing spiritual death in the life of the soul. This type of sin is contrasted to *venial* sin which weakens the soul, but does not destroy it. The Roman Catholic Catechism states:

> [1861] Mortal sin … results in … the privation of sanctifying grace, that is, of the state of grace. If it is not redeemed by repentance and God's forgiveness, it causes exclusion from Christ's kingdom and the eternal death of hell …

Mortal and venial sins are distinguished by the issue of will and involvement of the individual. When one commits a venial sin there is an inner conflict between what the person knows to be right and the sinful action being performed. "I know that it is wrong to steal, and I did not want to do it, but I did it." With mortal sin there is the total volitional and emotional determination of the individual which leads to the sin: "I will murder because I hate him!" So, in mortal sin the individual merely brings to light the type of person he is. The one who murders is a murderer by nature. Mortal sins can be dealt with through repentance and the Sacrament of Penance.

The Sacrificial Nature of The Mass

One of the primary issues that distinguishes both Roman Catholicism and Eastern Orthodoxy from Protestantism concerns The Eucharist— The Lord's Supper, Holy Communion. In Roman Catholic teaching, when the priest consecrates the bread and the wine, the elements are spiritually *transformed* into the very body and blood of our Lord Jesus. This doctrine is called *transubstantiation*.

Because of transubstantiation, The Mass—the formal celebration of the Eucharist—is viewed as a continued participation in the sacrifice of Christ. Although, most Roman Catholic theologians would say that this does not mean that Christ is being sacrificed over and over again, because Jesus' body and blood are physically present in the elements, His sacrifice in the past is continually linked to the actions in the present.

Justification and Sanctification

Aquinas taught that "Man is justified by faith, not in the sense that he merits justification by believing but in the sense that he believes *while he is being justified*" (Hannah, "to the Modern Era" 147 emphasis mine). Thus, classic Roman Catholic theology views *justification as the climax of sanctification,* the two being inseparable. This is very different from Protestant theology which sees Justification preceding Sanctification which produces Glorification. In other words, Roman Catholicism teaches that a person is not completely right with God until the end of the whole salvation process. The assurance of Salvation in the present time cannot be guaranteed in this view.

Although Roman Catholic theology affirms that salvation comes by grace through faith, this may be misleading to someone not familiar with the subtle theology behind the statement. Grace does come through faith, **but more faith receives more grace**. This is why The Sacraments are so important. The individual works *with* God's grace through faith and thus *cooperates* in salvation.

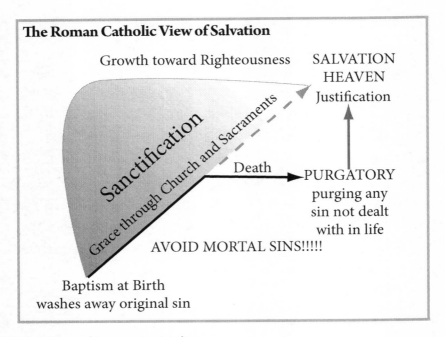

The Roman Catholic View of Salvation

Growth toward Righteousness · SALVATION HEAVEN · Justification

Sanctification

Grace through Church and Sacraments

Death → PURGATORY purging any sin not dealt with in life

AVOID MORTAL SINS!!!!!

Baptism at Birth washes away original sin

Devotion (And Worship) to Mary

Mary also takes a prominent place in Roman Catholic spirituality. Though the doctrines surrounding her were developed over many years, they were not finalized until the Second Vatican Council (1962-65). Stimulated by her alleged appearances in Lourdes, Fatima, Megigoria, etc., the council voted to devote a chapter to her in the Dogmatic Constitution on the Church. Six major points concern Mary:

1. **Theotokos**: "the one who gave birth to God" although this was originally an affirmation of the deity of Christ, it eventually became the avenue through which Mariology expanded;

2. **Mediatrix**: In the Middle Ages, Christ became a stern and unapproachable figure, therefore Mary became the sympathetic figure through whom the faithful could gain access to the Son. Mary becomes a mediator between the Christian and Christ;[7]

---

7   "Nothing is bestowed on us except through Mary, as God himself wills. Therefore as no one can draw near to the supreme Father except through the Son, so also one can scarcely draw near to the Son except through his mother" 1891 encyclical letter, Pope Leo XIII.

3. **Immaculate conception**: Mary was born without original sin;[8]

4. **Assumption**: Jesus keeps his mother safe from the corruption of the grave by taking her directly into heaven "to reign as Queen at the right hand of her son, the immortal King of the ages" Munificentissimus Deus, Pope Pius XII, 1950.

5. **Co-Redemptrix**: Although this term is avoided by Catholics, the idea is clearly present in the constitution of Vatican II: "(Mary) was united with (Christ) in suffering as he died on the cross" and cooperated "in the Savior's work of restoring supernatural life to souls."

6. **Mother of the Church**: "mother of all Christians." Pope Paul VI referred to her as "Mother of the Church" when declaring the results of Vatican II in 1964.

It is not hard to see why Mary has become the center of spiritual devotion for many Catholics. In some sense, Mary has become the *icon* of the Roman Catholic church. She is prayed to and she receives some limited forms of worship, although some might argue she receives complete worship. Because she is the mediator between the faithful and her Son Jesus, she is able to speed prayers to the Son.

Since the era of The Reformation, there has been a sharp division between Roman Catholic and Protestant theology. However, there *is* a common theology shared by the two. Both accept the doctrines of the virgin Birth, atonement, bodily resurrection, and Second Coming of Christ. Largely, conservative Protestantism has been reticent to give anything or anyone, outside of the Scriptures themselves, any binding authority over the community of believers. Catholicism, however, has allowed greater latitude in the use of tradition as a source for doctrine.

---

8 Anselm taught that Mary was born with original sin, Bernard of Clairvaux and Thomas Aquinas taught that she was conceived with original sin but was purified before Birth. Duns Scotus originated the dogma as it is stated today. "We declare, pronounce and define that the most blessed Virgin Mary, at the first instant of her conceptions was preserved immaculate from all stain of original sin, by the singular grace and privilege of the omnipotent God, in virtue of the merits of Jesus Christ, the savior of mankind, and that this doctrine was revealed by God and therefore must be believed firmly and constantly by all the faithful" *Ineffabilis Deus,* Pope Pius IX, 1854.

This is seen most clearly in the doctrines of the infallibility of the Pope and the veneration of Mary. It is also evidenced by the inclusion of the Apocrypha (a collection of extra books from the Old Testament era placed between the Old and New Testaments) in the Roman Catholic Bible.[9]

Roman Catholicism embraces the believer with a great respect for the holiness and "otherness" of God. This is one reason it continues to be a major spiritual influence in so much of the world. The strong distinction between the priesthood and the laity only enforces the mystical idea of worshiping God in holiness and order, while preserving a strong sense of the need for good works (and The Sacraments) in the life of the devoted.

---

9   The issue of the Apocrypha is a hotly debated issue even within some Roman
     Catholic circles. For a good overview see Norman Geisler and Ralph E.
     MacKenzie, *Roman Catholics and Evangelicals: Agreements and Differences.*
     Grand Rapids: Baker, 1995, pp. 157-75.

Eastern Orthodoxy

Eastern Orthodoxy has long ruled the eastern half of Europe, most notably in the Greek and Russian Orthodox churches. This tradition never really gained many adherents in the West especially after the Schism of 1054.

For those of us shaped by the Western Tradition (Roman Catholic > Protestant), encountering Eastern Orthodoxy feels like meeting a Martian. This tradition comes from a very different angle and sees things in a different light.

Eastern Orthodoxy is not a monolithic system. It is a communion of independent, self ruled churches, each typically governed by a Holy Synod. The Bishops which oversee these churches are considered equal by virtue of their ordination. Thus Eastern Orthodoxy has no central governing structure and does not organize around an "earthly vicar" as the Roman Catholic Papal hierarchy.

The Authority of Tradition

"Next to the Bible, the ecumenical councils occupy the highest place of authority in the church. All ecumenical councils ground the source of spiritual life in the Trinity (the common divinity and eternal relations between the Father, Son, and Holy Spirit) and the incarnation (the Son of God becoming human)" (Nassif 43-44).

All the paths of Orthodox tradition find their beginning in the Seven Ecumenical Councils in which the orthodox doctrines of the person of Christ, His eternal relationship to the Trinity, the relationship of His divine and human natures, and the relationship between his divine and human wills are all hammered down. "The church sees herself as heir to a unified, consistent and continuous tradition of faith that has been handed down from Jesus Christ to the apostles and church fathers through successive centuries" (Nassif 29).

You hear notes in this statement that sound very similar to those of Roman Catholic Apostolic Succession, but there is a key difference. In

Roman Catholicism authority is centralized in the Papacy; in Eastern Orthodoxy authority is captured and recorded in tradition:

> "It is impossible to understand the spiritual life of the Orthodox Christian apart from the doctrinal underpinnings that define the way he is to pray, worship, and conduct life. The Dogmas are those authoritative teachings of the Orthodox Church that pertain to salvation through Christ and the Holy Trinity. *Dogmas are derived supremely from Scripture and witnessed to through a chorus of voices in the church's tradition* (the church fathers, councils, liturgy, iconography, hymnography, and disciplinary canons) (Nassif 41 *emphasis mine*).

As you can hear, the final authority of Scripture is affirmed. However, as will become evident in the following discussion, tradition exerts a very powerful, if not equal, influence as Scripture. Because Tradition and Liturgy form such a large part of the Orthodox practice, it is recognized that there is a greater degree of Biblical illiteracy among Orthodox lay people.

The accepted traditions of the Eastern Orthodox church also form the backbone of the Canon Law which governs the life of the church. Initiates to the faith are taught the canonical regulations.

The Incomprehensibility of God and the Incarnation of Christ

Eastern Orthodoxy took its foothold in Russia in the ancient region of Kievan Rus (Kiev) under the rule of Prince Vladimir in the 10th Century. There is a story in *The Tale of Bygone Years* (also called *The Primary Chronicle*, a history from that time) that recalls how Vladimir sent ambassadors to various countries in to find a good and true religion for his people. They went to the Muslims and found no joy. They went through Europe and eventually to Rome where they found more pleasing worship, but no beauty. Finally they arrived at Constantinople where they experienced the Liturgy at the Church of Holy Wisdom (*Hagia Sophia*). At last they had found the treasure they sought. They reported back to Vladimir:

"We knew not whether we were in heaven or on earth for surely there is no such splendor or beauty anywhere on earth. All that we know is that God dwells there and their service surpasses the worship of all other places. For we cannot forget that beauty" (Nassif 27).

The story above illustrates a central idea that moves this tradition: *the experience of the incomprehensible God through the beauty of His glory made manifest on Earth.*

The way in which Orthodox theology has developed is perhaps one aspect that is most alien to modern Western minds. The orthodox fathers discussed and practiced two ways to knowledge:

1. **cataphatic** (*via positiva* - positive affirmations about God), and

2. **apophatic** (*via negativa* - assertions that negate what we know about God with destroying the ideas completely.

An Orthodox theologian would affirm that "God is love and loving," but also that He is not "loving" in exactly the same way we know and express love. His essence and ways in their purest form are far beyond our ultimate comprehension.[10] "Christians know God through this unknowing. They can grasp him but can never completely get their arms around him" (Nassif 42).

This affirmation/denial methodology results in the deep sense of *mystery* present in Orthodox practice. This posture of profound awe and reverence before The God who is unknowable in essence but known in Christ keeps the believer rooted in the reality: *God is God and you are not*!

None of this denies the use of logic and the mind in spirituality. As Bradley Nassif states, "Christ died so that we may lose our sins, not that we may lose our minds." Theology and the theologian are not defined in the Western concepts of academic study, but in terms of the pursuit of knowing Christ in His Trinitarian relationships. Theology is *lived doctrine.* Theology is the pursuit of God in faith and practice.

---

10   Here you see the influence of Neo-platonism; God is meditated on in His pure form outside of "nature" and the observable.

The incomprehensibility of God is linked inseparably with the incarnation of Christ—God the Son: "The Word became flesh and dwelt among us and we have seen His glory…" (John 1:14). Truth is not explored in the abstract of logical propositions so much as it is explored in interpersonal relationships: Father to Son to Spirit to humanity.

Because God the Son became Human, so now *deification* is possible through prayer, works of love and grace, and particularly through The Sacraments. *What is deification?*

The Doctrine of Deification

"God became man so that we might become God."
(Athanasius of Alexandria c. AD 296-373)

The doctrine of *progressive deification* is the main distinctive between Eastern Orthodox and Roman Catholic or Protestant visions of spiritual growth. Deification is the Orthodox equivalent to the Western doctrine of *sanctification* although it is somewhat merged with the doctrine of glorification.

Drawing on the creation of humanity in the "image and likeness" of God in Genesis 1:26, the Eastern Orthodox tradition teaches that in the Fall humanity lost the *likeness* but retained the *image*. Therefore, Christian spirituality is defined in terms of restoring the lost *likeness* of God through redemption in Christ. The Holy Spirit does this work by channeling the "energies" of God to the believer. "Through the incarnation and atonement humanity can become by grace what Christ was by nature" (Nassif 54).

This is not to say that the believer takes on the pure, unknowable essence of God Instead,

"…the Holy Spirit who proceeds from the Father rests on the Son and becomes his energies. We who are called to the imitation of Christ are likewise freed to manifest the energies of the Holy Spirit, who, by adopting us as sons of God, makes accessible to us the spiritual power which belongs to Christ.

In this way we can fulfill what is seen as the biblical vision, that those redeemed by Christ will be like gods (cf. Psalm 82:6)" (Bray "Deification").

Eastern Orthodoxy generally views sin and the need for atonement through a different lens than the Western Tradition. Through Neoplatonic influence, evil is defined as "non-being" and so sin is simply what is not moving toward perfection. Thus sin is the *effect* of death and finitude, not its cause (Bray "Eastern Orthodox Theology"). Salvation is viewed in terms of the *freedom from death* and not so much the *guilt* of sin.

This comes from the Eastern Orthodox interpretation of the Fall narrative in Genesis:

> "Unlike Augustinian interpretation of Adam and Eve, our first parents were not created in a full-grown state of physical and spiritual perfection in complete communion with God. Rather, humanity was more like a developing young child who is charged with growing ever more deeply into the divine likeness through the process of deification… Accordingly the fall into sin was not a drastic withdrawal from a perfected state. Instead it was a failure to achieve the original purpose of God set out for humanity. It was a departure from the path of deification" (Nassif 54).

Christ, in His incarnation and through His death and resurrection, conquered the Devil and the power of sin so that the faithful may become "partakers of the Divine nature" (see 2 Peter 1:4). The Orthodox believer is called back to the path of deification through a life of devotion whereby he/she is transfigured into the image of God. In the process of deification we do not become 4th members of the Trinity, instead we become *ourselves*—the people God intended when He shaped us to bear His image and likeness.

Liturgical Practice and Monastic Piety

> " 'the rule of prayer is the rule of faith' (*lex orandi lex est credendi*). True prayer reveals the true God. The very word orthodox signifies correct belief as well as correct worship. Doctrine is doxological.

Truth understood in the context of worship. Prayer and theology are inseparable and interdependent" (Nassif 28).

The Orthodox approach to faith is a *liturgical* approach which means it structures communal, public worship and devotion around traditional forms, methods, and materials that have been handed down through the ages. Liturgy melds theology with the practices of devotion and worship. It should not surprise us then, that Eastern Orthodoxy has the oldest written liturgy of any Christian tradition.

Placed centrally on the altar in Eastern Orthodox churches is *The Gospel Book* (or *Book of the Gospels*) which usually contains all four Gospels from the New Testament and often other liturgical readings. The book is not bound in leather (skins of animals represent death) but is often decorated ornately with a depiction of the Crucifixion on the front and the Resurrection on the back.

In liturgical structure, the Life, Death, Resurrection, and Return of Jesus forms the Gospel foundation upon which all other practices and teachings unite. Or as the modern evangelical Orthodox Bradley Nassif puts it, "The gospel is like the mountain on which all the trees of the forest are planted" (29). The "trees" being a reference to the other practices—liturgy, sacraments, doctrine, etc.

The Divine Liturgy of the weekly service is structured around the Death, Burial, and Resurrection of Christ. It has been compared to a mini Eastern service. The annual liturgical cycle is built around twelve major feasts that outlines a larger view of Jesus' entire ministry from His birth to his return.

Along with liturgical worship, Eastern Orthodox spirituality promotes two other distinct avenues of devotion:

1. **Veneration of Icons**: Icons are used as symbols to convey the essence of what is represented so that the believer has some impartation of Deity. "We become what we behold," so to speak.

2. **Devotional Meditation**: Worshipers are directed to meditate in order to have an experience of God upon which the believer may then reflect. (We will discuss this more under Mysticism.)

The veneration of icons is a practice linked with the writings of John of Damascus and Theodore the Studite. Again the philosophy behind this teaching is Neoplatonic in nature. Just as man is created in the image of God, so Christ is the image of the invisible God, therefore the believer will be transformed into the image of God's Son. To see Jesus is to see God, even though Christ is only the *image* of God.

Theodore argues that "an icon is a true representation of the person (*hypostasis*) of its subject, but that it has a different nature (*ousia*). An icon of Christ is thus able to bring the believer into direct contact with his person, but it is not an idol" (Bray, "Iconoclastic Controversy"). Therefore, in some way, the icon—though not to be worshiped—can teach or impart something about the nature of Christ to the believer. Icons are not limited to depictions of Christ alone, but may include likenesses of the great Saints of the Church. With the worshiper surrounded with icons, both in the church and at home, there is an immediate experience of the communion of the Saints.

As in Roman Catholicism, monasticism still plays a key role in the tradition as a whole. St. Anthony is often cited as the role model for those who would devote themselves entirely to the radical call of discipleship to Christ. But his life also becomes a key example among many that the way of devotion to Christ is one born out of *desire*, not out of seeking merit which some Orthodox theologians see as a key failing of Western Roman Christianity coming out of the Middle Ages (and still present today).

> "Anthony fasted because he was hungry to love God more; he prayed because he wanted closer communion with God; he contemplated so he could better fix his gaze on his divine spouse; he practiced silence because he yearned to hear God" (Nassif 49).

The basic idea of *example>imitation* permeates not just the life of Orthodox monks but is also at the heart of Orthodox practice, which is "caught more than taught." Local pastors care for their flocks through the services and also through counsel and confession. "Self-guidance" is warned against as a great danger as it opens the individual to self-deception.

Spiritual exercises and disciplines are prescribed as means to both experience God and promote deification. Fasting, praying, and serving the poor are key means to these ends.

Sacramental Devotion

"The nature of communion with God cannot be reduced to a list of propositions or spiritual practices that will automatically bring about the desired closeness to God and others. On the contrary, Orthodox spirituality is caught more than taught. It is relational more than legal. It is experienced more than analyzed" (Nassif 28).

Similar to Roman Catholicism, Orthodoxy teaches that The Sacraments are expressions of the mystery of salvation specifically given for the nourishment and healing of the body and soul. They all have life-giving virtue. "The sacraments are often called 'mysteries,' not because they conceal Christ, but because they reveal and make Him present" (Nassif 36).

Since the time of The Reformation, Orthodoxy has numbered seven Sacraments being influenced by the Roman Catholic opposition to Protestantism. There are some who say that The Sacraments, in keeping with older Orthodox tradition, should not be limited to seven:

"A sacrament happens whenever God's grace is communicated through the created order. In one way or another, everything in the church is a sacrament, including the whole of creation, everyday labor, homemaking, and a multitude of daily tasks…Indeed, the incarnation of Christ himself is the supreme sacrament of God's presence in the world" (Nassif 38).

Nevertheless, the seven "official" Sacraments of Orthodoxy are:

1. **Baptism:** Similar to doctrines of Roman Catholicism, baptism is seen as an infusion of God's grace to the sinner, the first step toward deification: "…the 'womb' of new birth in Christ and the 'tomb' where one dies to the power of sin through the Cross" (Nassif 38).

2. **Chrismation:** anointing with oil immediately after baptism which indicates the presence of the Holy Spirit for empowerment. Is also used to reconcile an Orthodox who left and returned to the church, or for Catholics or Protestants who join.

3. **Eucharist/Holy Communion**: The central act of worship this sacrament nourishes the faithful through *the real presence* of Christ in the bread and wine. Unlike the Roman Catholic *transubstantiation*, Eastern Orthodoxy teaches that the Holy Spirit descends *upon* the elements during the liturgical invocation.

4. **Repentance or Confession:** a sacrament of healing in which the faithful confesses his or her sins to Christ in the presence of a priest.

5. **Holy Orders**: the ordination of the priesthood/clergy which manifests and represents the saving actions of Christ to the congregations through liturgy, preaching, and various other methods.

6. **Matrimony**: a sacred relationship which represents the mystical union of Christ and the Church.

7. **Anointing the Sick**: the offering of communion by a priest to the dying. In recent times this has been expanded to include the anointing of the sick.

Emphasis is often given to the reality that these Sacraments do not work automatically, or mechanistically apart from faith. Instead, they represent *a collaboration between human will and God's grace*:

"It is an unequal emphasis in which God takes the initiative in saving grace; yet it is one that requires a response by human beings. The church recognizes that we are all saints by grace, but we must also become saints by our actions" (Nassif 39-40).

Eastern Orthodox spirituality largely remains an enigma to Protestants. However, Orthodoxy is making minor inroads into the West. This probably stems from the fact that many are looking for an expression of faith with *a solid and enduring tradition* behind it. For many, Eastern Orthodoxy provides an alternative view of Christianity that embraces more of their experience and spiritual union with God than other traditions.

Major Influence: Mysticism and Contemplative Spirituality

Although mysticism has been closely associated with Roman Catholic spirituality and even more so Eastern Orthodoxy, it is an approach that finds some form of expression in almost all the major theological traditions. In the Middle Ages, mystical theology was based on a personal experience of God with subsequent reflection and meditation upon the experience. This basic idea is common to all forms of mystical practice.

There is some aspect of mysticism present in the Church Fathers all the way from Anthony and the "Desert Fathers" to Bernard of Clairvaux. In its earliest expressions, mysticism centered around *contemplative* meditation—the complete focus of the individual entirely captivated by thinking on God. Classic mysticism, however, is embodied in the works of St. John of the Cross, Ignatius Loyola, Thomas à Kempis, Catherine of Sienna, and Teresa of Ávila where the pursuit of the *mystical union* with God by intense contemplation marks the highpoint of spirituality.

Some forms of mysticism teach that an experience of God must be sought in *isolation* from the world. Asceticism (the denial of all the "comforts" of life) helps one to take their gaze off the earthly and focus on the heavenly. Spirituality is achieved through devoting oneself to prayer, meditation, fasting and any of the other disciples that might catalyze an experience of the holy.

Some of these ascetics, however, believed that the only true way to experience the holy was through self denial in the service of others. True spirituality is not defined by removing oneself from the world, but through embracing the world's suffering by denying self-pleasure.

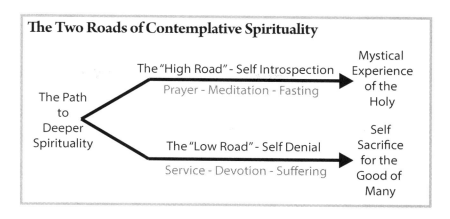

The Two Roads of Contemplative Spirituality

The mysticism that grew out of Roman Catholicism in the middle ages and continues to have an influence today centers around a *profound personal experience of God*. Mystic writers agree that the pursuit of this experience begins with a period of *purification* or *purgation*. The goal of this period is to achieve purity of heart.

> "What can we do to attain purity of heart? The answer to this is: surrender, abandon ourselves, submit, yield, humble ourselves, give ourselves over to God... Meister Eckhart spoke of 'total self detachment.' He observed *that the humble person has as much power over God as over self.* 'If this man were in hell, God would have to come down to him in hell,' he added" (Hinson 177-178 emphasis mine).

"The humble person has as much power over God as over self," has been reason for sharp criticism of some of these practices. Is the goal to submit oneself to God, or have God submit to the devotee?

When the contemplative denies the self, they become open to an invasion of the love of God that purifies and re-creates the worshiper into the image of God. This process is a painful process often called the "refiners fire." St. John of the Cross referred to this as the "dark night of the soul"—a time in which the worshiper is overwhelmed with the weight and grief of his sin and a feeling that he has been alienated by God. This "night" is divided into two halve: "the night of the senses" and the "night of the spirit."

"In the first, we may play a part in the purification of the senses, but in the second, love must take control, wiping out the last vestiges of the self-centeredness which prevents us from becoming one with God. As the fire consumes a log and turns it into itself, so God's love ignites the human soul and transforms it into love itself " (Hinson 180).

Through the practice of the spiritual disciplines (prayer, fasting, etc.) the worshiper then moves into a period of illumination reaching a peak in the *mystical union* itself. This "union" is not based on reason, ideas, or sensory functions, instead it is *supra-rational* experience.[11] This experience is often referred to in terms of a *spiritual marriage* as expressed in the thoughts of St. John of the Cross. These ideas have been made a bit more accessible in recent times in the song "Dark Night of the Soul" by Loreena McKennit:

Upon a darkened night
The flame of love was burning in my breast
And by a lantern bright
I fled my house while all in quiet rest

Shrouded by the night
And by the secret stair I quickly fled
The veil concealed my eyes
While all within lay quiet as the dead

Oh night thou was my guide
Oh night more loving that the rising sun
Oh night that joined the lover
To the Beloved One
Transforming each of them into the other

Upon that misty night
In secrecy, beyond such mortal sight
Without a guide or light
Than that which burned so deeply in my heart

That fire 'twas led me on
And shone more bright than of the midday sun

---

11   See Martin, "Mysticism" for more on this topic.

To where He waited still
It was a place where no one else could come

Within my pounding heart
Which kept itself entirely for Him
He fell into His sleep
Beneath the cedars all my love I gave

From o'er the fortress walls
The wind would brush his hair against his brow
And with its smoothest hand
Caressed my every sense it would allow

I lost myself to him
And laid my face upon my lover's breast
And care and grief drew dim
As in the morning's mist became the light
There they dimmed amongst the lilies fair.

Although this sounds like any love poem, it is not to be understood in purely passionate terms. The image is the experience of God's grace and love being poured into the person contemplating the mystery of the Holy One.

The union is a transference, in some sense, of the identity and understanding of the *One being worshiped* and the one *worshiping* (note: "*Transforming each of them into the other*"). The focus here is on the sharing of divine love. The worshiper is driven to a deeper love for God, the one worshiped, and this love takes control of the individual.

Hinson makes the analogy that this is the same experience of falling in love with another person: "You know what happens when you fall head over heels in love with someone. You can't get the beloved out of your mind. The beloved is present in every thought, shaping and directing every action" (172).

Because of the highly experiential nature of the mystic union and the understanding that comes from it, contemplative spirituality focuses largely on the care of the "inner life of the soul." Theology becomes the sharing, as best as possible, the content of the experience for the profit of those who seek such a union. Lossky comments, "If the mystical experience is a personal working out of the content of the common faith, theology is an expression, for the profit of all, of that which can be experienced by everyone" (9). This corporate outworking is reflected in the writings of mystics such as Catherine of Genoa, Catherine of Sienna, and Ignatius of Loyola.

Because of the largely individualistic approach of mystic/contemplative spirituality there has been little emphasis given to the ethical, social, or cultural expressions of Christianity implicit in the Gospel. Though not all mystics propose an *ascetic* lifestyle, the abandoning of all elements secular and common is at least encouraged by the nature of the pursuit of the mystic union. Truth is discovered in experience. The Bible becomes a guide to lead one to the experience of the union.

In more recent times, elements of mysticism have surfaced in the writings of Dietrich Bonhoeffer, Evelyn Underhill and especially the works of Thomas Merton. In Protestant circles the works of Richard Foster have reintroduced the ideas of the *contemplative life* to a largely evangelical audience.

Movements
in The Reformation Era

The era of The Reformation marked a time of upheaval and rediscovery for Christianity coming out of the Middle Ages. For over a thousand years, Western Christianity was dominated by the institutional mono-lith of the Roman Catholic church. However, as early as the 12th Century there arose individuals who began to question the practice of the Roman church. In 1517 Martin Luther would address 95 critical questions to the Roman Church and fan to flame an ember that had been smoldering for centuries.

Three major factors caused the tension that would result in the explosion of The Reformation:

1. The *authority* of the Pope to decide matters of eternal salvation
2. The *restriction* of the Holy Scriptures from the common people
3. The *separation* of the laity from the priesthood

By this time, the Roman church had become corrupt and oppressive. In "A letter to his pupil Grey," the great scholar Erasmus of Rotterdam jabbed,

> "Do not mistake me. Theology itself I reverence and always have reverenced. I am speaking merely of the theologasters [shallow theologians] of our own time, whose brains are the rottenest, intellects the dullest, doctrines the thorniest, manners the brutalest, life the foulest, speech the spitefulest, hearts the blackest, that I have ever encountered in the world."

Salvation had become a commodity that could be bought through the sale of *indulgences* (the pardon for sins committed or yet to be committed). This sale of indulgences fueled the massive building projects of the Popes in the "Dark Ages." Seeing the growing disparity between the clergy and the laity, many began to question the authority and practice of the Roman church. Many criticized that the Shepherds were slaughtering the sheep to build their kingdoms.

Since the Bible was not readily accessible to the commoner, there was really no means to question the authority of the powers that be on the basis of Scriptural Truth. In the era preceding the advent of movable type and the printing press, books were copied by hand and therefore very expensive. The Bible was copied more than any other book in this era, yet it was translated in Latin (The Vulgate, which the commoner could not read) and chained to the pulpit in the churches. There was really no necessity for the people to be able to read The Scriptures, the Roman church would argue, because they were not trained to interpret it. This was a job left to the Popes and the councils. Since the Pope and his prelates were more qualified to speak to matters of faith and piety, the people were guided and ruled by them.

In the 14th Century, John Wycliffe comes on the scene in England as one of the forerunners to the Great Reformation. He challenges the institution of Roman Catholicism by distinguishing the *institutional* church from *invisible* (true) Church. He also trains lay preachers (the so called Lollards) and sends them throughout England proclaiming the Gospel. In the early 1380s he produces the *first* English Bible. Although he was not the first to challenge institutional Romanism, he was one of the key sparks that would light the flame.

As the Vicars (representatives) of Christ, the Medieval Popes held great power not only in matters of religion but also in matters of state. Holding the keys to the gates of Heaven, the Pope could allow or deny entrance to those whom he chose. With the power to decide matters of eternal destiny, kings and princes generally submitted to the will of the Pope without question.

During the reign of the Roman church, salvation was seen as something to be *earned*; certainly not something that was freely given. Fear of eternal punishment and guilt became the tools that the Roman church used to keep both kings and peasants in submission.

In the late 1300's Jan Hus (John Huss) challenged Papal authority, the sale of indulgences, and the doctrine of transubstantiation. Hus could not be tolerated by the powers that be and he was burned at the stake in 1415 after the Council of Constance.

Although there were many "sparks" kindled before him, Martin Luther is generally regarded as the fire that set The Reformation ablaze. The epiphany that most affected Luther and the other reformers concerned the relationship between the gracious God of Scripture and sinful humanity.

Luther was plagued in conscience over his sin for most of his early life. In much of the art of the Roman church, Christ was portrayed as the stern Judge with a sharp sword coming from his mouth to punish the unrighteous. Terrified by this vision, Luther sought to be freed from the guilt of his sin by devoting himself to a monastic life.

As the Roman church taught, in order to be forgiven for a sin, you must confess it to gain absolution and ultimately forgiveness. This posed a logical problem for Luther. He reasoned that in order to be forgiven, you must confess. In order to confess you must remember the sin that was committed. If you cannot remember the sin, you cannot confess, therefore, you cannot receive forgiveness. Luther was plagued by this thought. He often confessed for hours on end.

Yet the more he confessed the more he realized an even greater problem: the more sin he confessed proved that he was *a sinner by nature*. How would a holy and righteous Christ forgive a confirmed natural sinner? Luther *despaired*.

Then the light of God's Word burst through. Luther had become a teacher of theology and thus had access to books that others did not. With these tools at his disposal Luther decided to do something radical. Instead of studying the Latin translations, he decided to return to the original Hebrew and Greek versions of the Bible. Luther was liberated by what he found.

As Luther was studying through the book of Romans he was plagued by the idea of God's *righteousness*. Luther understood God's righteousness to be *only* His right *to condemn guilty sinners* as the Roman church had taught him. Yet as Luther struggled with the book he made a startling discovery. Contrary to what He had been taught, Luther came to understand that no one could ever do enough to earn salvation. What is more, all of humanity is born bound to sin "in Adam" and apart from God's grace no one could ever hope to be saved. *The only requirement that God places on the sinner is to believe in His Son. By faith the sinner is made right with God.* Thus God's righteousness is not only his just judgment of sinners, but His righteousness to justify sinners through faith in Christ. *Luther would never be the same.*

At first, Luther and the other reformers only wanted to "reform" the Roman church. When this became impossible, they split apart from it entirely. This fact was cemented in 1521 when Luther burned the papal bull *Exurge Domine* which Pope Leo X had sent to excommunicate him from the church. Before his "enlightenment", the threat of excommunication and eternal condemnation would have terrified Luther. But now with his new found truth, the very gates of paradise had already been opened to Luther by Christ and he feared no man. The spark of reformation tendered by others before him was fanned into a blaze by Luther.

But The Great Reformation was not a unified theological front as many often assume. In fact there were several geographical fronts to The Reformation in Northern Europe—the German, Swiss, and English being the ones we will focus on

Aside from these geographical fronts, there are four main strands of Reformation theology that developed:

1. **Lutheranism** in Germany,

2. **Calvinism** or **"Reformed Theology"** under John **Calvin** in Geneva and Ulrich **Zwingli** in Zürich.

3. **Anglicanism** (The Church of England) in Britain

4. **The Anabaptists** (*As representatives of the Radical Reformation*)

Although the work of The Reformation was absolutely necessary in the bigger picture, it also raised a thorny theological problem that sticks with us today. The Roman church had reigned as the self-proclaimed sovereign dispenser of *The Truth* for the past 1000 years. This Constantinian/Christendom[12] model shaped all of Western Culture. So the question is, "If this source of authority proved false and corrupt, *how can we trust any authority figure from this point forward*? This question would ultimately lead to PostModernism.

To deal with the issue, the reformers replaced *the sovereignty of the Institutional Church* with *the sovereignty of God*. Jan Hus stated that the Pope was not the true "head" of the Church, only Christ Himself. Thus, truth is not tied to a human *institution*, but to God's self revelation *in* Christ and *through* His infallible, authoritative Written Word.

Although the different strands of The Reformation agreed on issues related to justification by faith and the primacy of Scripture, there was great dispute over the nature of The Sacraments (which many Protestants would now call Ordinances) and other doctrines. These disputes and disagreements would ultimately fracture Protestantism (those who "protested" the authority of Roman Catholicism) into a multitude of denominations and sects.

Historically, Calvinism has had a wider influence than Lutheranism. The theology of Calvin, Zwingli, Heinrich Bullinger and Theodore Beza set the stage for the birth of Covenant Theology which is fully developed in the writings of Johannes Cocceius and François Turretin. Many of these reformers died before they were able to complete a fully developed theology of sanctification and spirituality, along with other key doctrines like *Ecclesiology* (the study of the Church) and *Eschatology* (the study of last things). Their followers continued their work and reformation theology has flowered into several systems that continue to expand the tapestry of Christian spirituality.

---

12 "Christendom" (Christianity+Dominion) is the term that is often used to refer to the merging of Christian doctrine with secular power. Christendom ruled the West from the time of Constantine until The Great Reformation.

Lutheranism

In 1916, Theodore Engelder, a Lutheran scholar, published "The Three Principles of The Reformation: *Sola Scriptura, Sola Gratia, Sola Fides*." This article was one of the first attempts in the 20th Century to summarize the core principles which catalyzed The Reformation. *Sola scriptura* means the Holy Scriptures *alone* have final authority in the life and practice of the believer; *Scripture stands over Tradition. Sola fide* emphasizes faith *alone* as the instrument though which Christ's merits are received; *faith is the instrument of salvation, not works. Sola gratia* affirms that it is by God's grace *alone* that a believer merits the benefits of salvation in Christ; *grace supersedes merit.* Later two more were added *Solus Christus*—"through Christ alone," and *Soli Deo Gloria*—"for the glory of God alone." Each of these core principles stood opposed to key tenets of Roman Catholic doctrine.

For Martin Luther The Word (the Holy Scriptures) held great power. This power is revealed in two forms: Law and Gospel. The **Law** is that portion of the Word which convicts and condemns the sinner (and the believer as necessary), whereas the **Gospel** is that aspect of the Word which comforts, creates faith and saves the believer. Luther made a clear delineation between these two works in his exposition of Scripture. Since Christ had initiated a New Covenant of Grace and had, therefore, replaced the Old Mosaic Covenant of Law, the believer was to live a life ruled by the Gospel of Grace and not enslaved to the rule of Law.

The Sinner and The Grace of Christ

Luther rediscovered the New Testament truth that Christ is the gracious provider of salvation as proclaimed in the Gospel. At this point Luther stands strongly against the doctrine of the Roman Catholic church. Where Roman Catholicism teaches that justification is a state of grace in which good works gain merit (Aquinas), Luther countered with the argument that it is by *Christ's merit alone* that the sinner gains justification—right standing before God. The **Augsburg Confession** (the great Lutheran Confession) defines justification, "to absolve a guilty man and pronounce him righteous, and to do so on account of someone else's righteousness, namely Christ's." Therefore, justification is not based on anything done by the believer, but by the work of Christ *alone*. Therefore, the gift of salvation is based on an *unconditional promise* based in Christ's work. *Faith in Christ* is the only necessary requirement for gaining this promise. In this sense, the present salvation of the believer is based *on a legal declaration*. Although the believer is united and identified with Christ by faith, he or she, nevertheless, remains a fallen, sinful being in actuality.

Luther affirmed that the believer is *simul justus et peccator*—"at the same time just, yet sinful." The real issue in the spiritual life is not that we must become better behaved Christians, but that we must become people of *better faith*. Our righteousness is based on our relationship to God in Christ, not necessarily on our behavior. Sin, in this sense, is described as a "lack of faith":

> "We are simply declared just for Jesus' sake. But that means simultaneously that we are revealed to ourselves as sinners. The sin revealed is not just a misdeed, but it is precisely our lack of faith and trust over against the incredible goodness of God. The sin ultimately expelled is our lack of trust, our unbelief" (Lossky 23).

Justification Leading to Glorification

It is also clearly expressed by Lutheran theologians that faith clearly looks to the *perfecting* of the individual that will be accomplished in the process of glorification. Thus, faith is the instrument that allows us to see clearly the full scope of salvation. If the believer focuses only on their works and what they think they are producing, they will inevitably lose focus on the true goal and conclusion of sanctification: *Christ*.

> "Perfection is not sanctity but faith… It is a perfection of attitude rather than of achievement, of relation more than of realization, of truth more than of behaviour… It is not a matter of our behaviour before God the Judge, but of our relation to God the Saviour…

It is a fatal mistake to think of holiness as a possession which we have distinct from our faith... Every Christian experience is an experience of faith; that is, it is an experience of what we have not... Faith is always in opposition to seeing, possessing, experiencing. A faith wholly experimental has its perils. It varies too much with our subjectivity. It is not our experience of holiness that makes as believe in the Holy Ghost. It is a matter of faith that we are God's children; there is plenty of experience in us against it... We are not saved by the love we exercise, but by the Love we trust" (Forsyth).

Justification Leading to Sanctification

This is not to say that the issue of morality or practicing sin is irrelevant for the believer. The Christian experiences the struggle between the old sinful nature tied to the flesh (Adam), and the new nature that has been given through Christ. Here again the Word of the Gospel (which includes the "visible word" of Baptism and Holy Communion) works in the believer's life to sustain and recreate the believer in the image of Christ.

"The goal in Lutheran theology is to preach the Gospel of Christ and that preaching will by itself reform the sinner, but never completely... Since the believing Christian is never completely a believer, but is filled with doubts and the downright unbelief of the Old Adam who lives within him as an unwelcome and uninvited guest, the Christian in so far as he is still an unbeliever engages in works which must be labeled as clearly sinful for which he must face the consequences in this world" (Scaer 169).

Sanctification, therefore, is a work of the Spirit completed apart from the "good works" of the believer. *Justification is the source of sanctification.* And since justification is based entirely on the gracious work of God in Christ, so also is sanctification. For the Lutheran, good works do not produce sanctification; *sanctification produces good works.* Justification is not the final result of sanctification (as Roman Catholicism taught), it is the beginning of the work of God's grace in the life of the believer. *As such, spirituality is not maintained on the basis of good works, but on the effective work of the Holy Spirit in the life of the believer.* Therefore, sanctification is seen as the practice of getting used to justification:

> "Sanctification, if it is to be spoken of as something other than justification, is perhaps best defined as the art of getting used to the unconditional justification wrought by the grace of God for Jesus' sake" (Forde 13).

MANY forms of Protestantism imply or state explicitly that justification is more God's *part* of salvation, whereas sanctification is more the believer's *part*. In other words, God saves us freely by his grace (justification), yet we must show this to be true by good works (sanctification). Lutheranism in general would reject this idea.[13] *All* of salvation is left to the grace of God. For the Lutheran, to talk about sanctification as if it is something that *I* can produce in *my* life is very dangerous talk. One Lutheran commentator states,

> "[talking about sanctification in terms of something other than a gracious work of God] is something like bragging about prowess in love and sex. It is mostly hot air and rarely accomplishes anything more for the hearers than arousing anxiety or creating the illusion that they somehow can participate vicariously. We got started in that direction even in the above exercise in this thesis when we talked about how sanctification is "spontaneous," "free," "self-forgetful," "self-giving," "uncalculating" and all those nice things. Dangerous talk. Dangerous because, like love, none of those things can actually be produced by us in any way... And So at the very least, we can say that sanctification cannot in any way be separated from justification. It is not merely a logical mistake, but a spiritually devastating one" (Forde 16).

The relationship between justification and sanctification always entails the issues in the debate about the relationship between God's activity and man's. Just how do the Lord-God's sovereign desire and

---

13   Luther, in fact most of the reformers, never really finished their theological work particularly their understanding of sanctification. In this discussion we are looking at how the movement was expanded by Luther's followers and those who have been major proponents of the system.

power interact with the will and activity of human beings? *This is the key question that divides.*

Lutherans have challenged other Protestant forms of spirituality as simply being *moralism* based in the idea of good works gaining merit similar to the system proposed by Roman Catholicism. If spirituality is defined on the basis of restraint from sin then it becomes something which is measurable, and for the Lutheran smells too much like Romanism. Any teaching which seems to make the believer that actual instigator of good works is opposed.

So then, the process of sanctification can best be described as a process in which the believer moves from a state of unbelief into deeper levels of faith. The issue in this view is not obedience to the letter of the Law, but faith in the power of the Gospel. "Sin as a total state, can only be fought by faith in the total and unconditionally given righteousness" (Forde 26). Spirituality is defined in terms of depending on God's grace more and more. Spirituality is not,

> "...something the Christian can accomplish by his/her efforts. The Christian life becomes an if/then situation, whereas, in Scripture, it is a because/therefore arrangement. Faith is not a condition, it is a gift of God. Spirituality is by faith, not by works. This is radically different from the conditional thinking that is tied to the law where spirituality means cutting down on sin. The true Christian life begins when one realizes the simultaneity of sin and righteousness operating in him/her at any given time." (Houghton 5)

As the believer learns to depend more and more on God's grace the more the believer will hate sin and do good spontaneously, without calculation.[14]

---

14 "Fruits of the Spirit, however, are those works which the Spirit of God, who dwells in the believers, works through the regenerated, and which the regenerated perform in so far as they are reborn and do them as spontaneously as if they knew of no common, threat, or reward" Formula of Concord, Epitome VI, 5.

Of Faith and Good Works

Good works are defined in the Lutheran tradition primarily in terms of service to one's neighbor. Since the believer loves God, she will also love her neighbor which proves that she loves God. In this sense, Lutheran spirituality is not focused toward heaven but toward earth. By expressing love for the neighbor, the believer may "become like the original pair in Eden who knew God and His law in a positive light..." (Scaer 180). This is also worked out in the lack of distinction between secular/sacred in the life of the believer. A preacher is no more sanctified than a Christian janitor. Both vocations become instruments through which the believer, in faith, produces acts done for the good of the community. This again highlights the extremely positive emphasis in Lutheran spirituality: the important thing is not what the Christian *does not do*, but what he or she *does in faith*.

> "The moral life is the result of the old being's struggle to climb to the heights of the Law. Sanctification has to do with the descent of the new being into humanity, becoming a neighbor, freely, spontaneously, giving of the self in self-forgetful and uncalculating ways (Cf. Matthew 6:3-4)" (Forde 15).

As we have already seen, Luther defined the Law as something left over from the Old Mosaic Covenant which was made obsolete by the New Covenant in Christ. Yet for Luther, this does not mean that the Law has no benefit for the believer. The Law can be used to instruct the believer in holiness, but only if it is interpreted in terms of Gospel and not as Law. Sanctification, more specifically good works, is not produced by *negative prohibitions*—"Thou shalt not..."—but in *positive action*.

Therefore, simply restraining from sin does not necessarily produce sanctification. Even the unsaved can keep laws outwardly with the appearance of doing good works. In Luther's treatment of the Ten Commandments in his Small Catechism he interprets the first commandment, "You shall have no other Gods before Me" as a positive admonition for the believer to "fear, love and trust God above all things." He turns a prohibition into a positive admonition.

Christianity, the Lutheran would argue, cannot be "reduced to things permissible and illegitimate," instead the believer exercises positive faith in Christ through which the Holy Spirit produces good works (Scaer 168). All that the believer does is related to the work of Christ alive *in* the believer.

> "The Christian lives his life as belonging to God alone. Negative prohibitions in the moment of the Gospel and of faith are no longer necessary, since the Christian is alive to Christ and dead to sin and the law. By faith Christ is now living in him and he is no longer living, but Christ living in him… *The Christian or sanctified life is Christological, first of all because Christ lives in us by faith; secondly it is Christ who is doing these works in us; and thirdly these works are clearly recognizable as those which Christ alone can do and which He in fact does in us*"(Scaer 177).

Progress in sanctification or spirituality is not something that is necessarily outwardly quantifiable. Although growth is seen in terms of service and vocation, it cannot be presumed that these outward signs have a spiritual motivation. Growth is "growth in grace—a growth in coming to be captivated more and more, if we can speak, by the totality, the unconditional nature of God's grace" (Forde 27). Sanctification is not merely a "repair job" in which sin is battled, but it is more the invasion of a radical new life given by the grace of God in Christ to be received by faith. "That means we are being taken more and more off our own hands, more and more away from self, and getting used to the idea of being saved by the grace of God alone" (Forde 29). And the invasion of God's grace brings a marvelous change in the life of the believer:

> "Under the pressure of this total gift, we might actually begin to love God as our God, *our* God, and to hate sin. Think of it: We might actually begin to dislike sin and to hope for it's eventual removal. Ordinarily we feel guilty about our sins and fear their consequences, but we are far from hating them… It

is not that sin is taken away from us, but rather that we are to be taken away from sin—heart, soul, and mind, as Luther put it…

The grace of God should lead us to see the truth about ourselves, and to gain a certain lucidity, a certain sense of humor, a certain down-to-earthness. When we come to realize that if we are going to be saved, it shall have to be absolutely by grace alone, then we shall be sanctified. God will have his way with us at last" (Forde 29, 32).

Unfortunately, Lutheranism today has become more of a liturgical, sacramental faith contrary to what Luther would have probably wanted. But these realities were set in place by Luther's theology, particularly his views on Baptism and The Lord's Supper. Luther held to a form of "baptismal regeneration" that ultimately fought against his views on salvation by faith. This is seen most clearly in the issue of *infant baptism*. If a baby can receive the benefits of grace and salvation through baptism, then is faith absolutely necessary? Luther came to the startling conclusion that babies may exercise some form of faith even though being unaware. His inability to leave all forms of *sacramentalism*[15] behind would cause rifts both in Lutheranism and Protestantism in general. We will discuss this key issue more under the Radical Reformers.

Martin Luther is one of the most important men in Western history. Yet, he is a complex and controversial character. He had many failings but also many successes.[16] His legacy lives on in the lives of men and women who turn to The Scripture and there find the grace and mercy of God in Christ available through faith.

---

15 Sacramentalism is the view that God's grace is communicated and *transferred* through certain acts or objects and are therefore *necessary* for salvation.

16 Luther translated the entire Bible into German before the end of his life. Luther's German edition of the Bible standardized the German language. Not only did Luther translate the entire Bible, but by average he also wrote a book every two weeks of his life. *Luther was a giant in no uncertain terms.*

Major Influence: Pietism

The pietistic movement began within Lutheranism in the middle 1600's with the ministry of **Jacob Spener**. Oddly enough, within 100 years of their birth, both the German and Swiss sides of The Reformation had begun to decline. Concerned for the general corruption and complacency that had enveloped the Lutheran church subsequent to the Thirty Years War (1618-48), Spener and his followers called for a *reformation* of the Lutheran church!

Spener set forth his position for the reformation of the church in the *Pia Desideria* (*Pious Wishes*). He advocated for more use of the Scriptures among his people. Following Luther's lead, he advocated *the priesthood of all believers* by which *every* Christian should be involved in ministry. This was closely tied to his view of Christianity as a practical faith to be worked out, and not a mere collection of knowledge. He instructed his followers to be restrained and gracious when engaging in controversies and to love and pray for unbelievers and those who were living in error.

Spener led reform in the education of ministers highlighting the need for personal piety and devotion along with the standard academic subjects. These ministers were admonished to preach "down to earth," understandable sermons that connected with the people rather than academic discourses which few could understand.

Spener was soon joined in this endeavor by Hermann Franke who attempted to implement these ideas at the University of Leipzig. Franke became the organizer of Pietist ideas and was behind the founding of orphanages, Bible societies, and homes for women. Along with the work of Count Nicolaus von Zinzendorf and the **Moravian** church (which was instrumental in the conversion of John Wesley), Pietism has had a lasting influence on British and American Christianity.

Traditionally, conservative Pietism has followed Lutheran theology. The movement has stressed the preeminence of grace in justification and sanctification as opposed to the teaching that meritorious works accomplish these things in the life of the believer. The careful study of the Bible in the original languages, devotional reading, and the practical application of the Scriptures have continued to be major aspects of this movement.

> "In general, Spener and Franke attempted to walk the middle of the way between dogmatic rigidity and emotional warmth, between faith and works, between justification and sanctification, and between forsaking the fallen world and affirming it through love of neighbor, enemies and God's good creation" (Brown).

The Pietists argued that where, "Luther had reformed a doctrine, there must also be a *reformation of life*" (Brown). This reformation of life meant more of an emphasis on the *emotional* appeal of Christianity that makes a claim on the *affections* of the believer. It is not enough to seek transformation of thought; the desires and emotions must be addressed by God's truth and grace as well.

In this respect, there is a certain amount of *mysticism* often tied to the Pietist tradition, yet not as full blown as that discussed earlier. This led to early charges that the Pietists were too subjective in their views. Also, some strands of Pietism have developed a culture of *moralistic legalism* that may be just as harmful as *theological elitism*.

At the heart of Pietism is the call for reform *within* the Protestant church. Wherever theological coldness and doctrinal dogmatism has gained a hold, the Pietists have countered with the call to *practicality* and *morality* as expressions of Biblical truth.

> " …pietism was—and continues to be—a source of powerful renewal in the church. At its best it points to the indispensability of Scripture for the Christian life; it encourages lay people in the work of Christian ministry; it stimulates concern for missions; it advances religious freedom and cooperation among believers; and it urges individuals no to rest until finding intimate fellowship with God himself" (Noll "Pietism").

Reformed Spirituality

Although Lutheranism is considered a branch of *reformed* theology in that it grows out of The Reformation, *Reformed Theology* has come to be associated specifically with the work of **John Calvin** and **Philip Melancthon** in Geneva as well as **Ulrich Zwingli** and **Theodore Beza** in Zurich.[17] The Presbyterian churches are the primary contemporary expressions of this strand of spirituality. The Reformed tradition, however, has been the most influential movement coming out of The Reformation because most modern expressions of Christian spirituality trace part of their roots to this branch of The Reformation. This is due in large part to the fact that Calvinism was the most evangelistic of all the reformed movements producing over 21 creeds in as many countries.

Although John Calvin is closely associated with this tradition, it must be kept in mind that many of the developments within this movement that are still contemporary happened *after* Calvin's death. *Calvin laid the groundwork, his followers ran with it.* This is particularly true of Covenant or Federal Theology that grows out of the Swiss side of The Reformation. Today Covenant theology is almost synonymous with Reformed theology, but they are not one and the same (see the following section on Covenant Theology).

One of the early factors that helped forge classic Calvinist theology involved the dispute with the followers of Jacobus **Arminius** (1560-1609). A student of Beza, Arminius had become concerned that Calvin's followers were taking his teaching on election and Divine Sovereignty too far toward *fatalism*.[18] Arminius began to emphasize the human responsibility side of salvation. Arminius' followers devel-

---

17 Technically, all forms of Protestant theology are "reformed" (born in the period of The Reformation).

18 If everything is predetermined, man has no freedom and no real choice. Things simply take place because they must.

oped his initial work into a system of theology formulated in five points called **The Remonstrance**.

The first point said that man has *free will*. Man did not lose the faculty of self determination in the Fall and can choose good in the sight of God. *Conditional Election* states that God elects some people to salvation based on the fact that he knows (foreknowledge) *who will accept* the offer of the Gospel. Point three explains the death of Christ as a sacrifice that pays for the sins of the whole world and *makes salvation equally possible* to all people. The fourth point, *obstructable grace*, states that God's grace can be resisted by the free will of the individual. And finally, based on the conclusions of the other four points, the fifth point states that a person can *lose their salvation* by rejecting Christ in their free will. The Arminians and their teachings were condemned by the Synod of Dort in 1618-19. However, the Arminian doctrines would continue to have a strong influence in Protestant theology.

TULIP

In response to the Arminian's five points, the Calvinists formulated their five points. These essentials of Reformed doctrine have been summarized in the acronym TULIP which stands for T*otal Depravity, Unconditional Election, Limited Atonement, Irresistible Grace, and Perseverance of the Saints.* These points are exactly opposite to what the Arminians had proclaimed.

Total Depravity refers to the fact all of humanity, after Adam's rebellion, is born with the inability to please God—we are all sinners by nature. **Unconditional Election** refers to the teaching that God chooses some to be saved on the basis of His love, wisdom, and will alone and not for anything the believer does to deserve it. **Limited Atonement** is the doctrine which states that Christ did not die simply to make humanity savable in general, but that He actually redeemed the elect in His atoning work. **Irresistible Grace** and **Perseverance of the Saints** are related concepts which essentially state that God's work cannot be short-circuited by the actions of the believer—God is the one who initiates salvation, God is the one who completes it. *Once salvation is attained it cannot be lost.*

The Supreme Sovereignty and Providence of God

From these five elements, Reformed theology has developed it's larger doctrine of *sovereignty and predestination*. Although the emphasis on this doctrine has often been misunderstood by those outside this tradition (especially in relation to the writings of Calvin), it nevertheless remains an important part of the Reformed explanation of justification and sanctification. The necessity of predestination is rooted both in the character of God and the character of humanity.[19]

For Reformed theology, God is the Creator and Sovereign Lord of all creation over which He has complete and omniscient control. Humanity, however, has lost all ability to please the Creator by it's own initiative due to Adam's Fall and its effects. In order for a lost person to be saved, the *initiative* must come from God since humanity is "dead in it's trespasses and sins." God is the one who works to give the lost person not only salvation in Christ, but also the faith to receive that salvation.[20] In this way, the saved person can in no way claim any merit due to his or her actions or volition—*salvation is completely from God.*

When this is applied to sanctification, it becomes clear that God will finish the work begun in justification since the believer only responds to what the Holy Spirit is doing in their life to produce sanctification. In other words, if a person is *truly saved*, sanctification is a foregone conclusion. If the professed Christian does not see the out-working of sanctification in their life, then they might question whether or not they are truly saved. Even though the process of salvation is accom-

---

19 "Predestination means that human life is rooted in the will and the intention of God," John H Leith, *Introduction to the Reformed Tradition*, (Atlanta: John Knox Press, 1981), 104. God is at the center of all 'cause and effect' in the universe. He alone is due glory, therefore all things will (in the future) work together to show His glory. His will cannot be averted.

20 Scripture does seem to indicate that faith itself is a gift or provision of God. See Philippians 1:29 and 2 Peter 1:1. This point, however, is still debated even in Reformed circles.

plished solely by the grace of God, there are nevertheless "fruits" of this work in the believer's life.

The Holiness of God and The Depravity of Humanity

Reformed theology has always placed great emphasis on the glory, majesty and holiness of God. This is set alongside a very low opinion of humanity. This is due to the early reformers' heavy emphasis on the sinful nature of humanity created by the Rebellion and Fall of Adam. The doctrine of *total depravity* teaches that humanity in it's fallen state can in no way do *anything* to please God or win his favor (a view also held by Lutherans). This has pejoratively been called "worm" theology. We, as sinners, are just lowly worms in the eyes of a completely Holy God. Even after conversion, many older Reformed theologians argued, the believer continues to sin in many ways: "…man sins in his best as well as his worst deed" (Noll "Pietism").

God's great love is seen in that He sent his own Son to die for sinful humanity. So, in this sense, Reformed spirituality, just as Lutheran, is very Christocentric. All merit that accrues to the benefit of the Christian believer is given on the basis of Christ's work and not on anything the believer has done or will do. Justification is accomplished in the person of Christ. Sanctification is accomplished by *union with Christ*. The real struggle in the believer's life is with sin. In the life of the believer there must be the realization that once united with Christ through faith, the believer dies to the power of sin by being united to Christ's death.

> "We receive forgiveness of sins through Christ. This reception involves being united to Christ. The Christ to whom we are united, died to sin. Since we are united to Him, we also have died to sin. If we have died to sin, we cannot continue living in it. Therefore, we cannot continue in sin that grace my increase" (Ferguson).

The War Within

Initially, the Swiss side of The Reformation differed from the Lutherans over the nature of the Holy Communion, the use of The Law (specifically the Mosaic Law of the Old Testament), and several other key issues such as the nature of local church government. As it relates to spirituality, however, there are a couple of key issues which highlight the distinctive nature of this view.

Classic Reformed theology teaches that in every believer there is a *sinful impulse, principle, nature* which acts contrary to all that is good, holy and just, and also a *new impulse* or *new nature* which desires to do good. At this point there is some debate as to whether the believer has one or two "natures."[21] Some argue that there is only one new nature that is at war with old sinful desires. Others argue that there are two "natures" which fight in the believer like two dogs fighting over a bone.

Regardless of the semantics, in the end all agree that in some sense *the believer has become a new creation in Christ*. We have been taken out of the world created by Adam's sin and transferred into the kingdom of Christ, present and yet future. However, the sinful desires are constantly at battle with the spiritual desires of the Holy Spirit now present in the life of the believer. The "new" may not always win the battle. When the believer sins, it is due to the resurfacing of the "old sin nature" or "indwelling sin." The classic passage used to support this view is Romans 7:13-25. This conflict is inherent "in the very nature of the glory of what God has already done for us. The magnitude of grace, when it impacts fallen humanity in a fallen world, inevitably produces conflict" (Ferguson 61).

The remedy to this conflict is what Reformed theologians have referred to as *necessary mortification*. This is not the physical discipline and abuse of the body associated with medieval monasticism, but instead it is the putting off of the "old man/person" in Adam and the putting on of the "new man/person" in Christ. Mortification is based in our union with Christ in His death to sin and its dominion. This is

---

21 This whole debate is agitated by the notoriously difficult task of defining the term "nature." The Scriptures do not refer to a "new nature" or an "old nature" specifically and nor do they "nature" language to talk about these issues. Paul refers to the "new man/person" vs. the "old man/person" or the "desires of the flesh" which are at war with the "desires of the Spirit." The language and theological constructs that are often used in this debate make it necessarily difficult and unclear.

not just something worked out in our thoughts and desires but also in our behavior.

Calvin recognized in the New Testament an "internal and external mortification" (Ferguson 61). Mortification of the interior life consists in the continual reckoning by faith to be dead to sin through Christ, realizing who we are *in Christ*:

> "Sanctification is therefore the consistent practical outworking of what it means to belong to the new creation in Christ. That is why so much of the New Testament's response to pastoral and personal problems in the early church was: "Do you not know what is true of you in Christ?" (Cf. Romans 6:3, 16; 7:1; 1 Corinthians 3:16; 5:6; 6:2-3, 9, 14, 19; 9:13, 24) (Ferguson 60).

External mortification consists in resisting temptation, struggling with our sinful desires and the suffering and pain imposed on us through the providential experiences of life. Ultimately, the "new nature" will win out over the old:

> "Sanctification therefore, according to this representation, consists in the gradual triumph of the new nature implanted in regeneration over the evil that still remains after the heart is renewed" (Hodge III 224).

Although the struggle between the "old" and the "new" continues throughout the life of the believer, it will ultimately be resolved with the *imperfect* Christian being made *perfect* by glorification in Christ.

Positional and Progressive Sanctification

Reformed theology distinguishes between the *positional* (or *definitive*) aspect of sanctification and the *progressive* aspect of sanctification. *Positional sanctification* affirms the believer is made perfect and holy *positionally* by faith in Christ. So then a believer cannot become more "holy" since his/her holiness is granted through Christ and the work of the Holy Spirit. However, the believer is admonished to grow in light of this holiness. The believer is called to a life of growth and maturity in the knowledge and will of God. This *progressive* aspect of sanctification is accomplished through *the Word, the Providences, the fellowship of the local church, and The Sacraments (Ordinances).*

The **Word** is the primary means through which sanctification is accomplished. The ministry of the Word is practiced in *personal study of the Scriptures* and attending to *expository preaching*. The **Providences** are viewed as the sufferings, trials, and testings we endure in this life. These pains are the method God uses to shape us into the image of His Son. The **Church** is that fellowship of believers called out by God for salvation to be a caring and praying community. And finally **The Sacraments** (Baptism and the Lord's Supper)[22] are bound to the Word of God communicating to us and reminding us of the grace and love of God. Wishing to avoid the connection with *sacramentalism,* most Reformed and Protestant churches would now refer to these as *Ordinances*—rites commanded specifically by Christ.

Because this process of sanctification is controlled by the work of God in the Spirit, sanctification cannot fail:

> "Neither do those of reformed faith believe that the Christian can ultimately thwart the working of the Spirit in his/her life. The work of the Spirit in delivering the believer from the power of sin is executed by an unconditional, progressive, and irresistible work of the Spirit from the moment of regeneration. There will always be progress in a lifestyle of holiness for those who are truly 'saved.' If sanctification is not guaranteed, then the work of Christ and the word of God are rendered powerless" (Houghton 4).

The problem with this arrangement, as the Lutherans have charged, is that the spiritual life becomes one that can be outwardly quantified and not a matter of faith—trusting God to do what we cannot. There is always the question of "Is the Spirit really at work in my life?" "Is my spiritual condition getting any better?" On the outset it seems that this

---

22   There is a general rejection of *sacramentalism* in Reformed theology. The situation is complicated however. Most in the Reformed tradition would view the Lord's Supper as *symbolic* rejecting both Roman Catholicism's transubstantiation view and Luther's consubstantiation. Yet in the doctrine of *infant baptism* the tradition seems to affirm that God's grace and salvation is transferred in the ritual in some way.

assurance of sanctification when it is tied to justification would produce peace in the life of the believer knowing that God's work would not fail. Yet, the question often becomes, "How do I know that I am getting more spiritual?" Great emphasis, therefore, is placed on the means of Christian growth.

On the Uses of the Law

Although both Lutheranism and the Reformed churches held that The Law[23] was of benefit in the life of the believer, the Reformed tradition clearly has a much different emphasis in how the Law is to be used. Calvin held that the Law had three primary functions: (1) it shows the righteousness of God and the sinfulness of man (*convicts of sin*), (2) protects the community from unjust and evil men (*restrains evildoers*), (3) it teaches the believer how to live as it instructs us in the nature of God's will (*instructs in righteousness*).[24] This final use is the one most important to sanctification. The Law serves to show the believer what holy living is. It serves as a spiritual guide that reveals God's will in ethics, morality, and behavior in general. Hoekema states, "…believers are not free from the Law. They should be deeply concerned about keeping God's law as *a way of expressing their gratitude* to Him for the gift of salvation" (Hoekema 85 *emphasis mine*).

Contrary to the Lutheran position, Reformed theologians view the Law not as something just for the "Old Mosaic Era" but something that is to be kept *spiritually* by the Church. This has developed as a result of Covenant or Federal theology becoming intertwined with the Reformed tradition (*see discussion of Covenant Theology that follows*). Most Covenant-Reformed theologians view all of God's dealing with humanity after the Fall under the purview of the "Covenant of Grace" in which God is graciously revealing the particulars of living a life of faith.

---

23 Here we mean "The Law of Moses"—the commandments given under the Old/Sinai Covenant beginning with the 10 Commandments but entailing in some way all the other 603 commandments.

24 See Calvin Institutes 1.2.7: 6-16

In this sense, the Mosaic Covenant (the Law) is part of the gracious work of God just as the New Covenant in Christ.

In older forms of Reformed spirituality, this emphasis on the use of the Law has often resulted in a somewhat legalistic view. While this particular branch affirms the ultimate control and will of God in the process of sanctification, they have often stressed just as heavily the *obedience* of the believer to the Law. Hoekema summarizes the view this way:

> "The Christian life, we conclude, must be a law-formed life. Though believers must not try to keep God's law as a means of earning their salvation, they are nevertheless enjoined to do their best to keep this law as a means of showing their thankfulness to God for the salvation they have received as a gift of grace. For believers, law-keeping is an expression of Christian love and the way to Christian freedom; it is equivalent to walking by the Spirit. Since the law mirrors God, living in obedience to God's law is living as image-bearers of God. The Law, therefore, is one of the most important means whereby God sanctifies us" (Hoekema 88).

Reforming the Reformed

In recent years there has been a change in emphasis given to more classic representations of Reformed theology. Several theologians in the Reformed tradition (John Murray, Anthony Hoekema, James Martyn-Lloyd Jones) have claimed the title "neo-reformed." Within this movement there has not been so much a change in theology, as a change in the *emphasis* given to certain areas of doctrine.

The most prominent shift occurs in describing the Christian not as one person two competing natures or impulses, but as a truly regenerated person with *one new nature* in Christ.

> "We (believers) are now "in Christ." This means our self-image is positive rather than negative. There are not two equally powerful forces struggling in us. This awareness, that we really are a new person who can put off all these things of the old person, makes the Christian life actually possible rather than theoretical. Thus, we

are fully responsible for the production of the Christian Life (no more excuses of I did it in the 'flesh,' it is I who did it-good or bad) the commands and instructions in the New Testament assume that a Christian is wholly responsible for living the Christian life (Ephesians 4:22-24; Philippians1:2:12,13)" (Houghton 12).

Although the Christian still sins, sin does not control his/her life. The believer is no longer a slave to sin by nature since the new nature is created and rooted in Christ. Even though sin is not eradicated, in Christ the believer has the power to go for long periods of time without sinning. This is a somewhat radical departure from older Reformed thinking.

The Reformed tradition is important to study since it has had such a great influence on Protestant theology. Almost all forms of spirituality developing in the centuries following The Reformation have drawn on the works of the great Reformed theologians as the starting point for their own movements. The Reformed tradition has produced some of the greatest scholars in Christianity—John Calvin, Jonathan Edwards, and Charles Hodge to name a few. Because of its strong commitment to the Scriptures and holy living, the Reformed tradition has generally developed Christians of deep commitment.

However, as in all other traditions, "traditionalism" is an issue in modern Reformed churches. Many who have grown up in the Reformed faith do not know *why* certain doctrines are believed and practiced. A good friend of mine who was part of the Reformed tradition used to say, "Sometimes we have more faith in our faith than faith in Christ." This, again, is a danger in every tradition. Nevertheless, Reformed theology preserves an emphasis on certain facets of God's grace, power, and love that have been lost in more "modern" expressions of The Faith.

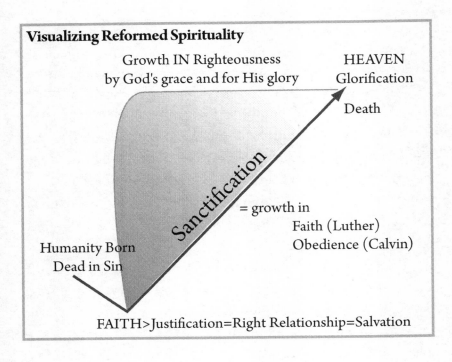

Visualizing Reformed Spirituality

Growth IN Righteousness   HEAVEN
by God's grace and for His glory   Glorification

Death

Sanctification = growth in
         Faith (Luther)
         Obedience (Calvin)

Humanity Born
Dead in Sin

FAITH>Justification=Right Relationship=Salvation

Major Influence:
The Radical Reformers and The Anabaptists

We have already seen how The Reformation was not a singular move-ment and revolution, but instead had several faces and fronts. The most extreme division existed between what is called the **Magisterial Refor-mation** and the **Radical Reformation**. The Lutherans, Calvinists, and Zwinglians (along with others) argued that the Church should work interdependently with the secular authorities—the *magistracy*—such as princes, magistrates, and city councils to promote the work of the Church. The Radical Reformers, like the **Anabaptists**, believed that there should be no overlap or direct interface between the church and the state due to the corruption it had produced in the Roman Catholic church. They also saw this corruption surfacing in the Lutheran and Calvinist sides of The Reformation.

The conflict between the Magisterial and Radical sides of The Reformation is one of the darkest periods of Christianity. For those on the magisterial side, the radical reformers posed a great threat to their vision of recovering a truly "Christian State" free of the corruptions of Constantinianism. One of the great sticking points between the two sides involved the issue of baptism, particularly infant baptism. In order to understand this conflict, we have to go back to the ancient church.

Although some argue that infant baptism goes back to the 1st Century and the Apostolic church, *clear evidence* of the practice dates only to the 2nd Century. The New Testament is silent on the issue, although some have inferred it's validity by "reading between the lines" in certain passages, particularly those that mention whole households being baptized.

It is clear, however, that by the 3rd Century infant baptism was practiced in the church as a *sacrament* (an infusion of God's grace) which washed away original sin from the infant. In AD 251 Cyprian counseled that the baptism of infants should not be delayed "lest in doing so we expose the soul of the child to the risk of eternal perdition"

(Lutzer 120). There is also clear evidence in the writings of some of the Fathers that by that time The Sacraments—at least Baptism and the Lord's Supper—were seen as being necessary and essential to salvation. They were not viewed as symbols, but as means that are necessary to salvation: *forgiveness of sins came through The Sacraments.*

After the Constantinian revolution began in AD 313, infant baptism became one of the cornerstone practices that would unite the authority of Church and State. If children could be Roman citizens by "accident" of their birth-place, then why could they not also be Christian by the providence of their parentage? Once Christianity had become THE religion of the Roman Empire, to be baptized, christened as an infant, was to be recognized as a Roman citizen. This was a major brick in building a "Christian-state" or Christendom as it is typically called.

The Donatists of the 4th Century were among the first groups to oppose infant baptism, but they were quickly quashed. In the time of Charlemagne (9th Century) others arose who would not practice infant baptism and argued that it should only be allowed for those who could consent to the Sacrament with understanding of the commitment. During this time adults who were *re-baptized* after personally coming to faith in Christ were put to death!

"The fear was that if the church was considered only a group within society rather than coextensive with society, the whole unity of church and state would be fragmented. Infant baptism was the 'glue' that united church and state" (Lutzer 123).

When we come to the 17th Century, the Anabaptists (which means "to be baptized again") once again challenged the doctrine of infant baptism along with other doctrines and practices. Their *literal interpretation of Scripture* often put them at odds with both the Magisterial Reformers and the Roman Catholics. Many of these radical reformers, taking the teaching of Jesus seriously, would not take oaths, participate in military actions or in civil government. Once again they were a threat not only theologically but also politically. *The were slaughtered in the thousands.*

There were some on the side of the Radical Reformation who fought back and advocated violence against their opposition. Thomas Münster was a leader of the bloody German Peasant War of 1524-25 in which around 100,000 poorly armed peasants were slaughtered. Others advocated non-violence and pacifism. Menno Simmons was one of the most influential leaders in this camp who also founded The **Mennonites**. The **Amish** and the **Hutterites** were two other pacifist, separatists communities that appeared in connection with the Mennonites during this time.

The impact of the Radical Reformation and particularly the Anabaptists was profound. Apart from the communities already mentioned, the Anabaptists are the roots in the family tree that produced the modern Baptist denominations. Key "modern" doctrines like the separation of church and state, the priesthood of all believers, and freedom of religious practice which shaped the course of the Western world, particularly the United States, were first championed by these "radical reformers" who challenged "the powers that be."

Major Influence:
Covenant Theology (Federal Theology)

Covenant or Federal theology is usually associated with Reformed Theology and more specifically John Calvin (1509-64) and Calvinism. Although the theology of Calvin did much to lay the foundation for the later development of this tradition, Covenant Theology was only fully realized after the death of Calvin in the works of Kaspar Olevianus (1536-87), Johannes Cocceius (1603-99), and particularly François Turretin (1623-87).[25] Covenant theology has also been closely associated with "5-Point Calvinism," although *the two systems are not synonymous*. Calvinism addresses theological issues of *salvation*, Covenant theology addresses issues of *systematic* and *historical theology*.

Basically, Covenant Theology teaches that God has dealt with humanity in history on the basis of Two Theological Covenants, The Covenant of **Works** and the Covenant of **Grace**. Some older Covenant theologians include a third covenant—the Covenant of **Redemption** —that was made in eternity past between God the Father and God the Son that provided the basis for the other two covenants worked out in history.

These theological covenants are defined as contracts between God (the superior party) and certain people (Adam, then the elect) in which *promises* are given by God that can be received only through the accomplishment of the *conditions* given in the covenant. If the covenant was broken then certain penalties would also be applied.

Before the fall, Adam was under the *Covenant of Works* which promised eternal life if he would obey God and not eat from the Tree of the Knowledge of Good and Evil (conditions). Adam broke this covenant when he ate from the forbidden tree and thereby forfeited the

---

25 Turretin's *Institutes of Elentic Theology* became the textbook for covenant theology and would not be replaced until Hodge's Systematic Theology appeared in 1872.

benefits of that covenant and was penalized with *death* (both spiritual and physical).

After the Fall, God has graciously dealt with his people (the elect) through the *Covenant of Grace* by forgiving their sins and empowering them to live for Him. The promise of this covenant is again eternal life with the only condition for fulfillment being faith in Christ. The penalty for this covenant is eternal death. In the Old Testament this forgiveness was affected by the *anticipation* of Jesus' death in the animal sacrifices of the Levitical system stipulated in the Mosaic covenant.[26] In the New Testament this covenant was realized in the work of Jesus—His death, burial, and resurrection.

It is important to note that these covenants are *theological covenants*; they are **theological constructs** derived from inference and speculation and are not specifically named in Scripture. These covenants are not to be confused with the actual, specifically named *Biblical Covenants*: the Noahic, Abrahamic, Mosaic, Davidic, and New. Covenant theologians would argue that the "theological covenants" give meaning and coherence to the biblical covenants.

This raises an important distinctive of Covenant Theology. Since all of the Biblical covenants are subsumed under the "Covenant of Grace" all of the biblical covenants are viewed to be essentially the same in nature and function, although being different in particular stipulations. In this sense, the Mosaic Covenant holds the promise of life to those who would keep the Law and continues to be a standard of conduct for believers even after the death, burial, and resurrection of Jesus.

Because there is no clear distinction made between the Abrahamic, Mosaic and New covenants and their fulfillment in Christ, some Covenant theologians have adopted what has been termed *replacement theology*. This argument states that since the Church is viewed as the vehicle through which God now blesses all nations (as promised to

---

26　Some Covenant theologians go so far as to say that everyone who was saved in the OT period was given a special revelation of what Christ would do in the future so that they might be saved.

Abraham) in the present time, the promises that were made to Israel as a nation are viewed as being fulfilled *spiritually* in the Church in the present age and in the age to come. The Church, in this sense, replaces Israel or becomes "spiritual Israel." This spiritual fulfillment is also applied to other passages in the OT so that some parts of the prophets are not viewed as being *literal* explanations of how God would fulfill His promises but merely symbolic representations of the spiritual ideals.

The *Westminster Confession of Faith* and catechism have become the most well known expressions of the ideas of covenant theology. In the 18th Century, Covenant theology became entrenched in the universities and seminaries of the North-East due to the teaching and works of men like Jonathan Edwards, Charles Hodge and Horace Bushnell. In recent times Louis Berkhof, J. I. Packer and R. C. Sproul have become the major voices of Covenant-Reformed theology.

Visualizing Covenant Theology	
(The Covenant of Redemption—In Eternity)	
The Covenant of Works	**The Covenant of Grace**
Adam > Fall	*Everything after the Fall...* *All the Biblical Covenants* *Noahic, Abrahamic, Mosaic,* *Davidic, New*

Anglicanism

The word Anglican comes from the medieval Latin phrase *ecclesia anglicana* that means the English church. According to Anglican legend, Christianity came to Britain in the First Century through Joseph of Arimathea—Yes, the same Joseph who buried Jesus! The famous Glastonbury Abbey is said to have been founded by him. Whether or not this true, it is clear that Christianity had made it's way to the British Isles at least by the Second Century.

Saint Alban is the first known Christian martyr in the British Isles, executed in AD 209. From the Council of Arles in AD 316 onward, the church in Britain existed as a part of the Western Catholic church. The complete history of the Church of England is beyond the scope of our purposes here. Instead, we will focus on the "modern" establishment of the tradition in the time of The Reformation.

The Church in England remained united with Rome until 1534 when the English Parliament declared King Henry VIII to be the Supreme Head of the Church of England through **the Act of Supremacy** one of the major turning points in Church History. Henry desired an annulment for his marriage which the Pope would not grant. This dispute aggravated the already growing tension between Rome and Northern Europe which had begun to question Papal authority and the "Constantinian" union of church and state whereby church policy directed state policy. When Henry did not get his way, he directed Parliament to make a clean break from Rome.

Although now separate from papal authority, the Church of England continued to maintain many aspects of Roman Catholic theology, particularly The Sacraments. The church transformed, however, during the reign of Henry's son King Edward VI. There were several phases in **The English Reformation** but by the late 1600's The Church of England had become a separate arm of The Reformation, linked to, but distinct from the arms of The Reformation led by Luther, Calvin, and Zwingli in continental Europe.

Breaking free of papal authority and the feudal system of the Middle Ages, the Church of England set an example for the idea of *national churches* which were shaped by the culture and distinctives of each nation, but holding to the common tenets and teachings of Christianity.

In 1604 the English church established the 39 Articles which shaped the trajectory of the development of the church. Although the articles are no longer binding today, they still played a significant role in shaping Anglican spirituality. Many Anglicans point to the Chicago-Lambeth **Quadrilateral of 1888** as the main core of Anglican identity. The Quadrilateral established four points of Anglican orthodoxy: 1) the **Scriptures**, which contain *all things* necessary to salvation; 2) the **Creeds** as the *sufficient statement* of Christian faith—particularly the Nicaean and Apostles Creeds; 3) The **Sacraments** of Baptism and Holy Communion; and 4) the **Historic Episcopate.**

As is common to Reformation theology in general, the Anglican church recognizes only two *Sacraments*: Baptism and Communion. The doctrine of the *Historic Episcopate* developed from the New Testament *episkopoi*—bishops or overseers.[27] The Anglican church practices an episcopal polity which places bishops over local geographic areas. These Bishops are said to derive their authority from an unbroken, personal, apostolic succession from the Twelve Apostles of Jesus. In short, the Anglican church keeps a hierarchical structure like Roman Catholicism, but like Eastern Orthodoxy rejects the general idea of centralized authority—one man at the top to rule all others.

Within the Anglican tradition, there are so called "high" and "low" churches. "High churches" are those whose beliefs and practices are more on the formal, traditional, and liturgical side with a resistance to modernizing the church. These "High churches" have much more in common with Roman Catholicism.

---

27 This group is mentioned in Acts 20:28; Philippians 1:1; 1 Timothy 3:2; Titus 1:7; 1 Peter 2:25.

On the other side, "Low churches" tend to be more open to contemporary ideas and modernization. In recent times, "low churches" are increasingly called "Evangelical Anglican" and "high churches" called "Anglo-Catholic." Although this distinction is most associated with the Anglican churches, there is also a "high/low" division within Lutheran, Presbyterian, and Methodist churches.

The Book of Common Prayer is one of the most notable contributions of the Anglican church. For high church Anglicans, The Book is a key expression of Anglican doctrine. As within older orthodox approaches, reliance on The Book derives from the principle of *lex orandi, lex credendi* ("the law of prayer is the law of belief"). The Book contains the fundamentals of Anglican doctrine: the Apostles' and Nicene creeds, the Athanasian Creed (which is now rarely used), the Scriptures arranged by The Lectionary), The Sacraments, the daily prayer, the Catechism, and Apostolic Succession set in the threefold division of ministry: Bishop, Priest, and Deacon.

In the present, **The Anglican Communion** exists as an international association of independent churches consisting of the Church of England and other national, regional churches sharing a common fellowship. The **Archbishop of Canterbury**, has a place of honor among the other bishops of the Anglican churches but does not exercise any authority beyond England. He stands as a unifying figure-head for the communion.

The churches of the Anglican Communion consider themselves to be part of the One, Holy, Catholic and Apostolic church linking them back to ancient orthodoxy. They are also often considered to be *both* Catholic *and* Reformed. For some, Anglicanism is a non-papal Catholicism. For others, it is a form of Protestantism without a figure-head like Luther or Calvin. Still for others, Anglicanism represents some combination of the two. A wide continuum of belief and practice exists in the Anglican Communion including evangelical, liberal and Catholic.

There is no single Anglican church with universal authority and each national or regional church has full autonomy although the individual churches are linked by a common loyalty to the central Anglican doctrines. The Anglican Communion is the third largest Christian group in the world, after the Roman Catholic and the Eastern Orthodox churches.

Anglicanism spread to many regions and countries as the **Episcopal church.** In America, the Episcopal church broke from the Anglican church at the time of the American Revolution but has since restored ties to the Anglican Communion.

The history and practice of the Anglican church is rich and complex and we have only scratched the surface here. It is an important tradition within Christianity and a link in understanding how the era of The Reformation leads to the Modern era. The practice of the Anglican church in England also sets the stage for the rise of the Wesleys and Methodism to which we will now turn.

Movements in the Modern Era

The various theological branches stemming out of The Reformation ruled the protestant theological landscape from the 16th to the 19th centuries. Yet with the coming of **The Enlightenment** (mid 1700s) and it's strong emphasis on science and reason, the theological realm—as well as those of art and science—was pushed into a period of radical reexamination and redefinition. As we speak of the Modern Era, we don't mean "modern" in the since of what is more advanced or developed, but in it's technical sense referring to the period beginning with the Age of Enlightenment and ending somewhere around 1960 in the birth of the **Postmodern Era**. In this section we are going to look at the development of spirituality beginning around 1750 with the work of John Wesley and move to the late 1800's to the Keswick movement.

With the promulgation of Enlightenment ideas in the 18th and 19th centuries there was a major shift in the way *truth* was both defined and understood. The direct *propositional revelation* of God—Christians believe that God has clearly spoken to us in His Son and in His Word—was replaced by *human reason* as the foundation for truth. In this era we see a greater emphasis given to human ability and achievement. This is the era of mass production, capitalism, and political freedom. As the scientists pushed the earth from the very center of God's creation to the fringes of an infinitely vast and expanding universe, so also the concept of "God" was shoved to the fringes.

Since the traditional Christian interpretation of life, the world, and the Creator could not be squared (or so it seemed) with what science was discovering, Christianity and the Bible became downplayed as products of the "non-enlightened" ages. As science began to give an explanation of the world in terms of purely natural mechanics, the necessity of a Prime Mover, a Creator who had started all things, vanished. *If the universe can create itself, the idea of God is not necessary.* Even if there was a God who had created the world, He had vacated the scene long ago (Deism). Although Christianity tried to fight these trends, it had largely lost the battle in general culture by the middle of the 20th Century.

The Bible as absolute, infallible truth also came under heavy fire during this period. Many critics began to maintain that the Bible was simply the work of men (with good intentions) but that is all. Jesus was a good moral teacher, but He was not God, much less *The Savior* in any objective sense. This intense criticism gave rise to the Higher Critical School of scholarship in Europe which sought to free the Bible from the corruptions of tradition that had plagued it for so long. When these men were through, they had gutted the most sacred beliefs of orthodox Christianity. This attack on the Bible gave birth to *theological liberalism*, a force still alive at the beginning of the 21st Century.

If the Bible were simply *myths* and *allegories* in the sense that it did not reveal true historical fact as the liberals were claiming, then there was never really a real man Adam. If there is no historical Adam then there is no original sin leading to the corruption of all humanity. If there is no original sin, then what is sin, really? If we can't define sin, then what is Jesus dying for? When you deny the "first Adam," you will also inevitably deny the "Last Adam."

Based on this line of logic the liberals charged that the Church has *misread* the Bible and *misinterpreted* it. All the stories it contains are there to lead us to personal enlightenment, to make us morally responsible people—and that is all that salvation is. Jesus is simply our great example of liberated humanity, not the Creator God to be worshiped and obeyed. Christianity simply becomes one of the "many paths to god" (however you define him, her, it, they, we?????).

Yet during this period there is also a strengthening and expansion of *conservative* Christianity. John Wesley stands out as one of the great practical theologians of the Church, expanding reformed theology at the same time reviving it's expression in the lives of people. Within two years of the bloody beginning of the French Revolution which threw Europe into turmoil, William Carey jump-started the modern missions movement with his book *An Enquiry into the Obligations of Christians to use Means for the Conversion of the Heathens* (1792).

During this period, however, conservative Christianity begins to drink too deeply from the well of philosophy and science. *Democracy* and the ideas of *freedom of the individual* take precedence both in political and spiritual life. The birth of the United States and the revolutions in France and western Europe proclaim the death of the old Imperial systems and enthrone the governments "of the people, for the people, and by the people." Majority rule and freedom of expression become the new arbiters of personal and social truth. None of these moves are bad in and of themselves, but once they become divorced from *transcendent truth*, they create the infection in which the 20th Century festers.

As we will see, most of the major influences in Christian spirituality during the 1800's moved to a more *subjective* approach in understanding the believer's relationship to God. Yet the flowering of this subjective approach really does not reach full bloom until the 20th century with the rise of Postmodern culture and its general disenchantment with modern, Enlightenment ideas.

Wesleyanism

John Wesley (1703-1791) stands out as one of the most influential theologians and practitioners in Christian history. Wesley never wrote a systematic theology and what we know of him comes through his personal writings and stories of others. John, his brother Charles, and George Whitefield are considered the founders of **Methodism**. Where John was the great organizer of this movement, Charles was the propagator of Wesleyan ideas through his great Hymns. One contemporary minster of the Wesleys stated:

> "It is well known that more people are drawn to the tabernacles of Methodists by their attractive harmony, than by the doctrine of their preachers… Where the Methodists have drawn one person from our communion by their preaching, they have drawn ten by their music" (Leaver 17).

The influence of John Wesley's theology, however, cannot be overlooked as a profound influence in the spread of Christian spirituality in early America.

The Heart Strangely Warmed

John Wesley is most well known for his "Aldersgate experience." While struggling with the issue of his salvation, he attended a meeting in Aldersgate street, England,

> " …where one was reading Luther's preface to the Epistle to the Romans. About a quarter to nine, while he was describing the change which God works in the heart through faith in Christ, *I felt my heart strangely warmed.* I felt that I did trust in Christ, Christ alone, for salvation; an assurance was given me that He had taken away my sins, *even mine,* and saved me from the law of sin and death" (emphasis mine).

Before this experience of "strange warming," Wesley had already been an active Anglican minister, even spending two years in Savannah, in the Georgia colony, as a missionary. The time there was an almost complete failure. Wesley preached the reality that Christ forgives sinners, but had a very difficult time *applying that truth to himself!* It was not until his Aldersgate experience that the love and grace of Christ broke through and Wesley received Christ's grace *for himself*. Needless to say this experience had a profound influence on Wesley. This experience also guided his theological reflections in the development of his distinctive theology of sanctification and spirituality.

The Rebel and Organizer

Wesley was considered a rebel and renegade by the Anglican church. From his journal dated April 2, 1739, Wesley records,

> "At four in the afternoon, I submitted to be more vile and proclaimed in the highways the glad tidings of salvation, speaking from a little eminence in a ground adjoining to the city, to about three thousand people" (Noll *Turning Points* 216).

At this time, it was illegal to preach outside the standard alloted times for worship in Britain. Wesley realized that those who needed the Gospel most were not those in the stale Anglican congregations, but the workers in the fields and mines. This outdoor preaching and traveling came to define Wesley's ministry. By the end of his life, it is estimated that he rode 250,000 miles on horseback and preached some 40,000 sermons. On average, that is 449 sermons every year of his life!

As already mentioned, George Whitefield is also considered one of the founders of Methodism. Whitefield's theology, however, was strongly influenced by *Calvinist* theology whereas Wesley embraced the *Arminian* doctrines of the Church of England. Wesley and Whitefield split over this issue and challenged one another harshly from that point forward.[28]

Preaching throughout Great Britain, Wesley helped form and organize small Christian groups that practiced personal accountability, discipleship, and practical (and *methodical!*) instruction in the Faith. He also sent out itinerant, unordained evangelists to travel, preach, and

---

28 Despite their vicious debate over Calvinism, in the end both men confessed love and respect for one another and Whitefield requested Wesley to preach his funeral which Wesley did and gave great praise to Whitefield.

care for the groups already established. Under Wesley's leadership, the Methodists became key voices for change and reform of many social issues of the day, including prison conditions and the abolition of slavery.

Perfected by Love

It is important to realize that Wesley builds largely on many of the great reformed doctrines and, in some sense, he views his theology as a completion of the reformed doctrine of sanctification. The Holy Scriptures are "ultimate and authoritative" where issues of doctrine were concerned. Although Wesleyanism has been criticized for placing too much emphasis on experience, Wesley affirmed that "experience … could *confirm* a doctrine of Scripture, but it could not establish a doctrine of Scripture" (Dieter 13).

Wesley also held to the reformed doctrines of total depravity and the utter pollution of humanity through the Fall. Yet the Wesleyan tradition breaks with the reformed tradition in the way these doctrines are explained and applied. Through the Arminian influence, Wesley believed that although all men are fallen, God had given *common grace* to all so that the individual is able to receive or reject salvation. This is different from more Calvinistic teaching which states that God grants *specific*, saving grace only to those He has chosen.

The key idea that best summarizes Wesley's presentation of spirituality is "faith that works in divine love." Wesley, contrary to Augustine and the Reformers, defined The Fall not in terms of perversion, or lack of faith, or disobedience, but as a *lack of love*. This stems from Wesley's understanding of humanity's creation in the image of God. For Wesley there were three aspects of the image:

> "(1) *The natural image,* which gave men and women immortality, free will and affections; (2) *The political image,* which gave them the authority to rule the natural realm; and most important, (3) *The moral image,* by which they were imbued with righteousness and true holiness and were like their Creator in love, purity, and integrity" (Deiter 23).

The Fall affected the Image in all three of these areas, but the one which was most damaged and becomes the center of salvation and restoration is the third aspect: the moral image.

Whereas Wesley held strongly to the idea of justification by faith alone, just as Luther and the Reformers before him, his truly distinctive teaching resulted from a synthesis of Calvinism and Arminianism. Wesley agreed with the Calvinists that salvation was left entirely to the work of God in Christ through the Holy Spirit. But through God's common grace, the will of mankind is enabled to choose good or evil. Wesley stops short, however, of Arminian teaching with his emphasis that prior to conversion this *exercise of freedom results only in choosing what is evil or contrary to the will of God.*

Salvation becomes *primarily* the restoration of the third aspect of man's fallen image in that the believer is once again given the ability "to choose otherwise what he would not" (holiness, goodness, righteousness) (Hannah "in the Modern Era" 32). The Gospel gives the fallen person the ability to choose his/her destiny. This grace, however, does not guarantee that the person will always choose what is good. Grace also brings freedom and it is true freedom which may choose either good or bad.

For this reason, Wesley denied the idea of "the perseverance of the saints" (eternal security, "once saved always saved") taught by the Calvinistic Reformers. Since the believer was truly free, he could choose, after having a real expression of love and salvation, not to continue in the process of salvation (sanctification). In this sense, Wesley understands the act of justification being linked inseparably with *progressive sanctification.*

In his exposition of justification and sanctification, Wesley wedded the Reformed emphasis of God's sovereign grace with the principle of saving faith as an active principle of holiness in the heart and life of the individual. As Deiter states, "…the supreme and overruling purpose of God's plan of salvation is to renew men's and women's hearts in His own image" (17). So somewhat like Roman Catholicism, Wesley presents salvation primarily as a process of continual sanctification until one reaches perfection. However, unlike Roman Catholicism, this act begins with justification and terminates in glorification. *One achieves a right relationship with God in justification that must be maintained by sanctification.*

The Controversy of Perfection

As a means of accomplishing this end, Wesley believed that part of the promise of salvation was the removal by God of willful sin in the believer's life.[29] Wesley preached that the Christian should not be "content with any religion which does not imply the destruction of all the works of the devil, that is of all sin" (Dieter 13). Contrary to most other traditions during his time, Wesley believed that the continual struggle between "old and new natures" or between "the new nature and old impulses" was a common part of the everyday experience of the believer. Wesley argued that the remedy for this inner struggle lay in what he called *entire sanctification.*

Wesley's doctrine of *perfect* or *entire sanctification* is defined as:

"...a personal, definitive work of God's sanctifying grace by which the war within oneself might cease and the heart be fully released from rebellion into wholehearted love for God and others" (Dieter 17).

To this day, this teaching has remained the center of much debate and controversy. Since the older Reformed theologians had constantly maintained that the believer, even though justified, remained polluted by the sin of the Fall, Wesley's doctrine of perfection raised quite a stir.

Largely, it seems that Wesley's original teaching has been misunderstood by those outside the tradition and corrupted by those within. Apparently, Wesley did not intend to teach that the believer being

---

29 Wesley grounded this argument in passages such as Deuteronomy 30:6; Psalm 130:8; Ezra 36:25, 29; Matthew 5:48, 6:13, 22:37; John 3:8, 17:20-21, 23; Romans 8:3-4; 2Corinthians 7:1; Ephesians 3:14-19, 5:25-27; and 1Thessalonians 5:23.

made perfect ever reached a state of "sinless perfection." This is seen in the clear emphasis given to the necessity of daily growth:

> "…there is no perfection of degrees, as it is termed; none which does not admit of a continual increase. So that how much soever any man has attained, or in how high a degree soever he is perfect, he hath still need to 'grow in grace,' and daily advance in the knowledge and love of God the Savior" (Wesley quoted by Dieter 14).

Furthermore, this *relationship of perfect love* was not accomplished by moral effort but by the same faith in Christ and his work that had initiated salvation in the first place.

So then, it seems that in its purest form, *entire sanctification* was not meant to imply "sinless perfection," *but the perfection of love that overrides the power of sin in the believer's life.* Two main points of Wesley's philosophy are presented in this point: (1) the believer is restored to the image of God primarily by the renewed ability to love God and thereby resist sin, and (2) this exercise of love is *based* in the work of Christ, yet *made effective by* the free choice of the believer.

Much of Wesley's teaching and preaching was *moralistic.* Morality, however, was not an end in itself. It was as we have just seen, the result of living in *perfect love.* In one sermon on perfection Wesley defined it as consisting in:

> "1. To love God with all one's heart and one's neighbor as oneself; 2. To have the mind that is in Christ; 3. To bear the fruit of the Spirit (in accordance with Gal. 5); 4. The restoration of the image of God in the soul, a recovery of man to the moral image of God, which consists of 'righteousness and true holiness'; 5. Inward and outward righteousness, 'holiness of life issuing from holiness of heart' 6. God's sanctifying of the person in spirit, soul, and body; 7. The person's own perfect consecration to God; 8. A continuous presentation through Jesus of the individual's thoughts, words and actions as a sacrifice to God of praise and thanksgiving; 9. Salvation from all sin" (Dieter 18).

True Christianity, for Wesley, was simply to live according to the mind of Christ. The believer is to love God with all his or her heart, soul, and strength as well as his or her neighbor. Real freedom in the believer's life is not so much the *freedom from* guilt and fear of punishment, but the *freedom to* love God freely with the love that God Himself "sheds abroad in our hearts by the indwelling of the Holy Spirit."

> "There is 'nothing higher and nothing lower than this… love governing the heart and life, through all our tempers, words, and actions… Christian perfection is purity of intention, dedicating all the life to God. It is giving God all our hearts… *The Saving Christ is not a proposition to be accepted, but a Person to be loved and obeyed"* (Dieter 28).

Although, Wesley's teaching of entire sanctification has all but disappeared from the Methodist churches, there still remains a high moralism which can be directly linked to this doctrine. By and large the Methodist churches have strayed far from Wesley's theology. Many have become more liberal, denying the authority of Scriptures, focusing on societal concerns through the "Social Gospel." There is however a revival of fundamental Wesleyan ideals in the Confessing Movement within the denomination.

There is still a certain amount of moralism present in this tradition with a heavy emphasis on personal devotion and prayer, the results of which flow out in the service of the community. Wesley's "faith that works in Divine love" still remains a clear call to commitment in this tradition. Although John Wesley has largely become a forgotten figure in Christianity in general, his monumental contribution to the tapestry of Christian spirituality still lives in several traditions that sprang out of his influence. Aside from his theological influence, Wesley also stands as a key figure in the rebirth of the Apostolic, missional ministry of the Church—taking the Gospel to those who have not heard—which was mostly lost by the institutional church during the middle ages.

Major Influence: Revivalism

Generally revivalism has been defined as an appeal to the emotional nature of individuals for the need of salvation with the belief that "... vital Christianity begins with a response of the whole being to the Gospel's call for repentance and spiritual rebirth by faith in Jesus Christ" (Deiter "Revivalism"). Although this is not an accurate definition of all forms of revival, it still conveys the basic idea of what is communicated by the concept today.

The beginning of revivalism in this country is usually traced to the **First Great Awakening** which had its roots in Puritanism and Pietism. The movement began in 1725 with the preaching of Theodore J. Frelinghuysen in northern New Jersey. **Jonathan Edwards** and **George Whitefield**, however, are usually considered the two great preachers and catalysts of this awakening.

Both Whitefield and Edwards stood firmly in the Calvinist tradition which had exerted great influence in the American Colonies. The revival erupted in 1733-34 through the preaching of Edwards in Northampton, Massachusetts. The movement of the Spirit continued as Whitefield began his itinerant preaching circuit of the American colonies in 1738 after entrusting his ministry in England to John Wesley. The revival would continue into the 1740's and leave a lasting impact on Christianity in America.

Some have suggested that the great revival of the First Awakening should be credited to the dynamic preaching of the revivalists. This could hardly be the case with Edwards. Being almost blind, he read every sermon from a manuscript held inches from his nose in a dry monotone that could hardly be described as dynamic. Although Whitefield had more homiletic flair than Edwards, the results and lasting nature of this great revival are generally contributed to the direct work of God's Spirit in these communities.[30]

---

30   Although we have mentioned George Whitefield only in passing several times now, most historians agreed that he was the most influential preacher and

Edwards claimed that he actually did nothing different during this period than he had in the past. Instead, he with other pastors in the area, had become concerned with the general spiritual decline in their towns and began to pray, asking God to revive His people. The events that followed astounded even the ministers who had asked for this revival.

> "When revival came there was little doubt that it was the work of God rather than the work of men. Churches were filled and crime disappeared. Sinners sought out pastors to learn the way of salvation. This did not last a few weeks or months, but years" (Houghton 10).

The same cannot be said of **The Second Great Awakening** (1790-1840), however. Although this movement probably did begin as an actual work of God in Hampden-Sydney and Washington College in 1787 and in some of the "Camp meetings" associated with this move-ment, it is now clear that "methods" were what produced the spiritual awakening of the period. The preachers in the First Awakening had given a clear proclamation of the Gospel, with Biblical illustrations, and a "time of waiting for the mercy of God" to fall on the audience. The preachers of this second movement relied on *emotional manipulation* through *stories* to call the sinner to an *immediate decision* and *conversion experience.*

Charles G. Finney is the theologian most closely associated with the results of this Second Awakening. Although he probably should be seen as coming at the close of this movement rather than actually being a part of it, he nevertheless built upon the "methods" that were initiated by the movers of this Awakening.

Finney's theology has been labeled a "created anomaly" which rejected many of the orthodox tenets of classic Reformation theology. He has, however, remained a key figure in many modern denomina-tions. He never denied the Written or Living Word, but he gutted prac-tically everything else:

---

theologian of the 18th Century and made a lasting impact on the evangelical movement within the West.

"Charles Finney, the revivalist of the last century, is a patron saint for most evangelicals. And yet, he denied original sin, the substitutionary atonement, justification, and the need for regeneration by the Holy Spirit. In short Finney was Pelagian.[31] This belief in human nature, so prominent in the Enlightenment, eliminated the evangelical doctrine of grace among the older Protestant denominations…" (Horton "Crisis" 17).

Most of Finney's "new methods" were based in psychological and mental pressuring more than a call for the sincere work of the Holy Spirit. Finney himself denied the need for the supernatural in revival:

"A revival of religion is not a miracle, nor dependent on a miracle in any sense. It is a purely philosophical result of the right use of the *constituted means*—as much so as any other effect produced by the application of means" (Finney 5).

In reality, Finney simply capitalized on the mass marketing appeals produced by the flowering of modernist ideas in the business world of the day. *Emotional Manipulation* became the new science as well as the new theology and Finney was it's grand expositor.

Some of Finney's methods included a protracted meeting which wore down both the body and the mind. Those on the verge of "making a decision" were called to the "anxious bench" on the front row. Long emotional prayers and organized choirs were used to produce the proper psychological atmosphere. And of course, all the proceedings were socialized through the modern devices of advertising.

Around 1835, Finney became associated with Oberlin College and it's first president Asa Mahan. "Oberlin Theology" and "new methods" revivalism are synonymous with Finney's movement. This movement also saw the union of New School Calvinism[32] and Methodist

---

31 Pelagian refers to the teachings of Pelagius who claimed, contrary to classic Augustinian teaching, that a person can make the initial steps in starting his/her salvation—it is not a matter of God's special grace. Pelagianism was condemned as heresy in the Council of Ephesus 431.

32 This school is associated with the work of Nathaniel Taylor in which a new emphasis was given to revivalism, moral reform, and ecumenism. The major shift occurred with the introduction of semi-Pelagian doctrines.

revivalists. In the time between 1835 and 1875 revivalism took on a slightly different emphasis with the *perfectionist* teaching of Walter and (more notably) Phoebe Palmer.[33] The Palmers, Wesleyan Methodist by theology, introduced Finney to the *perfectionist* teaching and thus **Holiness Revivalism** was born.

In this synthesis, the revivalists began to call for a "second crisis of faith" (what the Calvinist branch called the "second conversion," "rest of faith," or the "higher life" and the Methodists called "entire sanctification," the "perfection of love," or "the second blessing"). The "second crisis" eventually became the "fullness" or "baptism" of the Holy Spirit associated primarily with the **Pentecostal** movement.

Dwight L. Moody dominated the revivalism scene from 1875 to 1899 in America. In this era, there was much more organization and greater budgets given to the "crusade" as it had come to be known. Whereas Finney had only begun to use the methods of mass marketing, the movers of this time exploited this new media to its fullest. Ira Sankey developed gospel music as an effective tool in the crusade and forever established the close association that has lasted to this day.

In Britain during this same era, **Charles Haddon Spurgeon**—a Calvinist who became known as "the prince of preachers"—shocked and awed attendees of the Metropolitan Tabernacle with his dramatic performances. Responding to one critic, Spurgeon said,

> "I am perhaps vulgar, but it is not intentional, save that I must and will make people listen. My firm conviction is that we have had enough polite preachers" (Galli 103).

Billy Graham is probably the best known revivalist of the 20th Century. He, however—like Moody and Spurgeon—rejected the aberrant (*heretical*) theology of Finney. The works of men like Moody, Spurgeon and Graham shaped the course of Evangelicalism, by modeling the use of *persuasion* in concert with the *clear preaching* of the Scriptures in *dependence* upon the supernatural work of the Holy Spirit.

---

33 The period from around 1850 to 1900 has been labeled by some as the **Third Great Awakening** due to the explosion of social reforms during this time.

Although Finney's methods have brought much criticism to revivalism, the work of God in a true revival should not be overlooked. Several characteristics have been suggested that mark a true revival like that of the First Great Awakening:

1. It is not the direct result of an organized effort by man, it is a providential work of the Spirit,

2. It is catalyzed as the *Word is preached faithfully*,

3. It *begins small and local* and spreads slowly (a movement),

4. It is *not sensational and commercial*,

5. It *produces a healthy fear of God* rather than shallow excitement,

6. It causes *confession of sin* and *renewed zeal* for God,

7. It *results in evangelism* as God's people are refreshed.

The negative effects of "fake" revivalism cannot be overstated.

> "Revivalism is detrimental to Christians because it is based on the assumption that we are not able to live a normal spiritual life so we need to be stirred occasionally to be lifted to that higher plane of existence. My understanding of Scripture is that the Christian life can be lived in the daily activities. If a person is morally pure, fulfilling his/her family duties, work responsibilities, worshiping and serving Christ, he is experiencing all there is to the Christian life. There is no higher level of super-spirituality that one attains by praying, witnessing, giving, or reading the Bible more. The whole revivalistic mentality is negative and operates by inflicting guilt" (Houghton 10).

Although revivalism is not a separate denomination or organized tradition, it nevertheless plays an important role in the development of Christian spirituality. Most notably it provides the link between Wesleyanism and the two other primary movements that come out of it: **Keswick** (pronounced kez-ick) spirituality and **Pentecostalism** both of which we will examine later.

Restorationism (The Disciples of Christ)

The term "restorationist" is a title that applies to a fairly broad range of traditions. The Christadelphians, The Millerites, The Latter Day Saints (Mormons), The Adventists, The Worldwide Church of God, Jehovah's Witnesses, and Plymouth Brethren are all "restorationist" movements which seek to restore *primitive* (1st Century), *simple* Christianity. The theology and practice of the different groups often share very little in common—the Plymouth Brethren are a conservative, orthodox group, whereas some of the other groups, like the Mormons and Jehovah's Witnesses, are considered heterodox, cultic sects.

We are going to focus here on the Disciples of Christ and the Christian Churches, with the Church of Christ being an offshoot of these two early branches. This branch of the restorationist movement is traced back to the work of Barton W. Stone, Thomas Campbell (1763-1854) and his son Alexander (1788-1866).

Initially, this movement had no desire to found a new church or a new denomination. Instead, "their purpose was to call all Protestant Christians to unity through the proclamation of the Gospel in its original purity" (Gonzalez, II 242). Alexander Campbell became the leader of this movement after he immigrated to the US from Ireland to join his father's ministry in the Christian Association of Washington (Pennsylvania). Early tension arose between Barton Stone and Campbell over how unity was to be achieved. Stone, being somewhat pietistic, argued that unity could be achieved in four ways:

> "1) head unity-all Christians learn to think alike; 2) book unity-all Christians agree on what Scripture means; 3) baptism unity-all Christians agree on the significance of baptism; 4) fire unity-all Christians experience the work of the Holy Spirit. He said the first three would never work, while an experience of the Holy Spirit could produce unity" (Houghton 11).

Campbell, however, disagreed with these ideas. Having received some education at Glasgow University before immigrating, Campbell combined *Lockean rationalism,* a profound respect for *the New Testament,* and *democratic idealism* as the framework for his attempt to return the church to *primitive Christianity* as he understood it. The newly won liberty of America and the strong nationalist spirit of late 18th, early 19th Century would be the soil in which this movement would grow.

Like many other Christians at the time, Campbell drunk deeply from the new found well of liberty. In fact Campbell wrote that July 4, 1776 was, "a day to be remembered with the Jewish Passover… This revolution, taken in all its influences, will make men free indeed" (Noll *History* 152). Yet this new liberty brought with it at times a deep resentment for the prevailing theological authorities. The grand reformation concept of *sola scriptura* (the Bible alone) was quickly transformed to "no creed but the Bible." "This blend of Christianity and democracy created a Christian message specifically adapted to the shape of American social realities" (Noll *History* 151).

Liberty for Campbell and his movement meant *peeling away* the corruptions that had encrusted the church and *returning* to the way the Apostolic church had existed. Scottish rationalism heavily dominated Campbell's thinking. Rejecting any forms of mysticism or piety he sought to interpret the New Testament rationally. This led to a strong insistence on the literal nature of the writings as well as an insistence to apply *all* teachings directly to the church.

Campbell's system of understanding salvation has been explained by the formula *Facts + Faith + Feelings = Salvation.* Facts are rooted in the truth of the Bible. Once these facts are known they are to be received by faith and in some sense, the facts give birth to faith. The emotions and feelings are not neglected but they must follow and proceed from faith built on the facts of God's Word.

In large part, Campbell was reacting to the forces of revivalism which were sweeping through Christianity in his day. Whereas the Methodists (later Finney) were placing strong emphasis on the *emotional element* of salvation and sanctification, Campbell called believers to a strict obedience to the teaching of the New Testament. He "rejected the excessive emotionalism which accompanied the supposed receiving of the Holy Spirit in the revivalism of his day, and taught that the distinguishing mark by which believers could know they had received the Holy Spirit was water baptism" (Houghton, 11).

For Campbell, baptism was an act of obedience to Christ's command and a means of receiving a specific absolution or effective release from guilt. This doctrine of *baptismal regeneration* became a defining point of Campbell's legacy as well as an example of the type of "ultra-literal" hermeneutic that was to be applied to the interpretation of the New Testament. But this sacramental view of baptism was nothing new; both the Roman Catholics and Reformed Protestants held to some form of this view at least as it relates to infant baptism.

Concerning the 1st Century church, Acts 2:42 states, "they were continually devoting themselves to the apostles' teaching and to fellowship, to the breaking of bread and to prayers." This pattern was imitated by the churches established by the followers of Campbell. The Lord's Supper is observed each week in the meeting, and originally there was emphasis placed on the strict observance of Sunday as "the Lord's Day." Spirituality for the followers of Campbell became defined by a pattern of obedience to the strict interpretation of NT principles.

The devotion of the movement soon revolved around the idea that if it is not specifically taught in the New Testament, then it is not to be practiced. For this reason, later developments of this movement banished all instruments from the worship of the church since they were not specifically mentioned as present in the assembly. But even things admonished in the NT were filtered through Campbell's Scottish rationalism giving some of his teachings an almost Deistic shape.

Little, if any, emphasis was given to the so called *spiritual disciplines* by Campbell. Again, due to his rational approach, Campbell reacted to anything that seemed to be "mystical" or "pietistic." This is seen clearly in the attitude toward prayer. The believer is to pray because it is commanded in the NT, yet the prayer has no power to sway God, or influence His action—God does not intervene *because* of a believer's prayer. Instead, prayer is more a response to the cause/effect laws that God has placed in the universe. This approach, in effect, stripped away an affective rationale for prayer and centered it in an acceptance of God's "providence" which Campbell defined as the order that God has given to the world.

Sanctification, then, becomes more an issue of obedience than anything else. The believer seeks to be obedient first to the word of The Scriptures, primarily the New Testament. This obedience is exercised in the weekly participation in the assembly of believers and in the "Lords Table" (communion). The life of obedience is begun with baptism through which one receives "the remission of sins" (Acts 2:38). The sanctified life is continued in the avoidance of sin by obedience to God's will as revealed in the NT.

In later developments of this movement (particularly the Churches of Christ), the strict literalism of Campbell's hermeneutic expanded into an admonition to strict obedience to NT "principles." It is not uncommon to hear sermons concerning the length of men and women's hair, the unacceptable nature of women wearing jeans, the evils of music, etc. in the ultra-conservative wing of this movement. The Disciples of Christ churches have largely abandoned these strict teachings for a more liberal theology. The Christian Churches, remaining for the most part conservative, have taken a mediating position between these two extremes.

Unfortunately, this movement (as all the other restorationists) failed to achieve the great goal of unity that Campbell had in mind. Because of a lack of internal structure this movement has become one of the most fragmented in North American Christianity. Although Campbell and his followers had no intention of starting a new denomination, this is exactly what happened. Furthermore, the more conservative and separatist elements of this tradition have largely withdrawn from dialogue and fellowship with other denominations due to a hyper-dogmatism by which they claim to be the only true expression of *the* Church. *The Lord of the Church seems to love irony.*

Major Influence: Dispensationalism

The end of the 19th Century was a very turbulent time within conservative Christianity. Since The Reformation, Covenant-Reformed theology and the hermeneutics[34] that supported it, had dominated the academic scene. However, the rise of *Premillennial Dispensationalism* in the 1800's would challenge the status quo. With the work of John N. Darby and C. I. Scofield, Dispensationalism gained a wide acceptance among the common people.

By the middle of the 19th Century, liberalism (fueled by the modernist worldview) had taken a strong hold in the seminaries and universities that were founded as schools to train Christian ministers. Schools like Harvard and Princeton became embroiled in battles for orthodoxy. At the heart of the battle were issues related to *how the Bible was to be interpreted.* The liberals were proclaiming that the Bible was nothing more than myth and human invention. Men like Charles Hodge stood opposed to these ideas and fought against them in their teaching and publications.

Another battle over interpretation was brewing not only between the conservatives and the liberals, but also *within* conservatism. The Covenant-Reformed theologians had been proclaiming that due to Israel's total rejection of their Messiah, Jesus Christ, the promises made to Israel in the Old Testament were going to be fulfilled "spiritually" in the New Testament Church. This conclusion also led some Covenant theologians to view the Church as the replacement for national Israel, thus becoming "spiritual Israel."

Many passages from the Old and New Testaments were read in light of a "spiritual fulfillment" principle grounded in the replacement of Israel by the Church. The "spiritual fulfillment" principle also linked with an *amillennial* or "realized" eschatology within Covenant/Federal theology. This brand of covenant theology taught that just as the Church had become "spiritual Israel" so also Christ was now reigning

---

34   Hermeneutics are the methods and means used to interpret the Bible.

"spiritually" over the earth and would not return to establish a visible earthly kingdom, but to usher in the Eternal Kingdom. The interpretation of Revelation 20 and the mention of a 1,000 year reign of Christ was the epicenter of this debate.

Before we go further, it is important to understand the significance of this Millennial debate. Revelation 20 states that Satan will be imprisoned and Christ will reign on the Earth with his Saints for 1000 years. What does this mean? And when does this happen? There are three options:

1. PreMillennialism: the view that Christ will return *before* (pre) the beginning of the 1000 reign.

2. PostMillennialism: the view the Christ will return at the *end* (post) of the 1000 reign which will be accomplished spiritually through the Church.

3. AMillennialism: the view that the 1000 year reign is *symbolic* and refers to the time between Christ's ascension and His return.

Although there is great debate over which view the early church held, there is evidence that many of the Church fathers held some form of Premillennialism (referred to as *historic premillennialism*). Others seemed to reject it. By the time of Augustine, Postmillennialism held sway as the growing Roman church in the West "conquered" more and more territory. By the time you get to Luther and the Reformers, Amillennialism takes hold as a more symbolic interpretation of the Bible becomes common.

Although its roots reach back to the 17th Century, Dispensationalism does not take its place as a major theological movement until the work of John Nelson Darby (1800-1882). As a minister in the Anglican church, Darby had become increasingly disturbed by the corruption and apathy that he saw in the denomination. In 1828 he left the Anglican church declaring it to be in ruins[35] and joined with the Plymouth Brethren—a nondenominational, restorationist group

---

35 Darby actually confessed the he believed most of the organized denominations had become the 'hand tools of the devil.'

which met in homes for Bible study and spiritual edification. During this period Darby developed an elaborate historical system for interpreting the message of the Bible as well as a strong emphasis on the necessity of a future, earthly reign of Jesus the Messiah.

Based on Darby's early work, Dispensationalism places emphasis on a method of *historical-grammatical, literal interpretation* of the Bible.[36] This distinctive led to three primary points of departure from the traditional Covenant Reformed position: 1) the Old Testament covenants were not fulfilled "spiritually" in the Church but would be fulfilled at some point in the future to national Israel, 2) the Church began on the day of Pentecost and was not present in the Old Testament, and 3) that Jesus would return to rule for 1,000 years on this earth in a period called the Millennium (*premillennialism*).

Dispensationalism is developed around the framework of an *historical-theological construct*[37] which is used to interpret the Bible. This methodology is one of the key features that distinguishes this approach from Covenant Theology. Whereas Covenant Theology seeks to explain the flow of Biblical revelation through the "theological covenants," Dispensationalism seeks to explain the flow of Biblical revelation through *historical eras*.

Classically, seven "dispensations" or "administrations" were put forth as the tools to "rightly divide the Word of Truth." Unlike the theological covenants, the dispensations were defined by how God gives,

---

36 This does not mean that the Bible is to be interpreted without reference and recognition of figures of speech and poetic language. Instead, this model seeks to understand the text as it would be understood by the original audience recognizing poetry and figurative language as expressions that do have objective truths behind them.

37 The "theological covenants" and the "dispensations" are both **constructs**. Though both are founded on general principles observed in Scripture, neither of the two arrangements is specifically named are referred to by Scripture. The Sacred Text does not specifically mention a "Covenant of Works" just as it does not describe the time between the Fall of Adam the Flood "the dispensation or administration of conscience." Although constructs are not inherently wrong, great care must given to make sure they are based on clear logic and adequate biblical principles.

takes away or expands His revelation *progressively in history.*[38] These dispensations were defined as that of:

1. Innocence (from creation to fall),

2. Conscience (from Fall to Flood),

3. Human Government (Flood to Abraham),

4. Promise (Abraham till Sinai),

5. Law (Sinai to Christ),

6. Grace (Christ till His return),

7. The Millennium (the 1,000 reign of Christ on the earth prior to the coming of the Eternal Order).

The concept of a *dispensation* dates as far back as Irenaeus in the 2nd Century. Other Christian writers and leaders since then, such as Augustine of Hippo, Francis Turretin (one of the "fathers" of Covenant Theology!), and Isaac Watts suggested certain historical, "dispensational" schemes in their teaching. Even the Westminster Confession of Faith notes that there is only one covenant of Grace worked out "under various dispensations"!

As it relates to spirituality, Dispensationalism views the relationship of the Old and New Testaments in a very different light than does Covenant theology. Covenant theologians had taught that the OT and NT were bound together by the common theological "Covenant of Grace."[39] This led to the deduction that the Mosaic Covenant was really just as much a gracious and binding covenant on the Church as was the New Covenant. As we have already seen, the Covenant-Reformed theologians generally view the keeping of some part of the Mosaic Law as an act of gratitude and obedience for the work that Christ is doing in the believer. Dispensationalists, however, view the Law very differently.

---

38 The concept of *progressive revelation* is also a key tenet for Dispensationalism. God did not reveal everything all at once, but gradually throughout history He has made His plans known little by little. Thus the Apostle John knew more about God's purposes than Abraham or Moses.

39 Covenant theologians affirm that these 'covenants' are not specifically mentioned in Scripture, but they can be *deduced* from certain contexts (cf. Louis Berkhof, *Systematic Theology*, p. 211ff.).

Dispensationalists view the Mosaic and New covenants as essentially different covenants in nature, purpose and fulfillment.[40] With the inception of the New Covenant with Jesus' death, Dispensationalists have argued that the reign of the Law has been brought to an end (Hebrews 8:7-13) and the New covenant is distinguished from the Old Mosaic Covenant in that the Law of God is written on the heart and not on stone (Hebrews 8:10). In other words, the Law is not to be kept *as a covenant stipulation* as it was under the Mosaic code.

Many dispensationalists argue that trying to keep the Law externally only results in more acts of sin (Romans 7:14-20; 1 Corinthians 15:56). The Law does still give revelation about the holy character of God, but it is *no longer enforced as a covenant stipulation* for the people of God. Instead, the believer *fulfills* the requirements of the law by living *by faith expressed in love* in light of the work of Christ. Where righteousness is pursued, sin is extinguished.

Dispensational theology becomes closely associated with the Keswick and Fundamentalist movements of the 20th Century. Within conservative Christianity a strong division still exists between Covenant-Reformed and Dispensational theologians. Within Dispensationalism there are divisions over some key interpretive issues.[41] Nevertheless, Dispensationalism has had a profound impact on evangelicalism in America through the popular teaching of men like D. L. Moody, Donald Grey Barnhouse, and Charles Ryrie. The Scofield Reference Bible, The Ryrie Study Bible and Dallas Theological Seminary rooted dispensational theology deeply in American culture in the second half of the 20th Century.

---

40   Dispensationalists, especially in recent years, have based their understanding of the *biblical* covenants on other, analogous ancient near eastern covenants. The Abrahamic, Davidic, and New Covenants are viewed as *covenants of grant* which are *unconditional* and *permanent*. The Mosaic Covenant (and The Law) is another form of covenant based on *obligation* and therefore temporary.

41   There are three major strands of Dispensationalism: Classic, Traditional, and Progressive.

The Keswick Convention

In 1875 several hundred men and women converged in the town of Keswick (pronounced without the *w*, *kez-ick*) England. The goal of this informal convention was to promote practical holiness by means of Bible readings, addresses, and prayer meetings. Although the meetings were stirred up by the spiritual fervor enveloping England in the revivals of D. L. Moody (with his choirmaster Ira Sankey), the founding of this convention is linked directly with an Anglican, Canon T. D. Harford-Battersby, and a Quaker, Robert Wilson. The convention has been closely linked with the ministry of Robert Pearsall and Hannah Whitall Smith. Asa Mahan (a close associate of Charles Finney) and W. E. Boardman (who wrote *The Higher Christian Life*) were also early associates of the Keswick meetings.

As explained in Hannah Whitall Smith's book *The Christian's Secret to a Happy Life,*[42] the believer should not lead "an existence of gloom and defeat," but should "walk in unbroken fellowship with God" (Pollock 6). The believer is urged to look beyond living an "ordinary" Christian life in the struggle between the old sin nature and the new nature controlled by the Holy Spirit. The *Secret,* Hannah reveals, is the joy that comes *through* and *from* complete obedience to Christ.

Originating in the Wesleyan teaching of the "second blessing" or "entire sanctification," the Keswick movement lays great stress on the *consecration of the believer by the filling of the Holy Spirit.* This consecration experience occurs sometime after conversion, at a time when the believer is earnestly seeking the will of God for a "higher life" of spirituality. This "filling of the Spirit" is not to be confused with the "second work of the Spirit." The "filling of the Spirit" is usually defined as a yielding by the believer to the power of the indwelling Holy Spirit who is ready and willing to lead to believer to maturity.

---

42   This book is still a popular classic and reveals Hannah's unique mix of her early Quaker roots and it mysticism, Plymouth Brethren doctrine, and a view of sanctification shaped by the Wesleyan-Revivalist movements.

The Truth in the Right Order

All who speak at these conventions (which includes preachers and scholars from several divergent denominations) give their addresses according to a set order and agenda:

Monday: The Holiness of God is contrasted with the sinfulness of humanity; a deep conviction for sin is promoted.

Tuesday: God's provision for victorious living is presented in an explanation of the finished work of Christ and union with him; a heavy emphasis is given to Romans 6-8 where the believer is said to be free from slavery to sin.

Wednesday: Consecration is presented as the response to sin and God's work in Christ; "unconditional surrender" to God is called for.

Thursday: Life in the Spirit is presented as the means to a victorious life over sin and "supernatural service" to God; here a distinction is made between being "full" of the Holy Spirit (i.e. controlled by), and "filled" with the Holy Spirit (i.e. "a special endowment for a particular occasion" of service).

Friday: Christian service is presented as the natural outpouring of a "Spirit filled life" and is shown to be the responsibility of the believer; A strong emphasis is given to missions.

Canon Dundas Harford-Battersby, the vicar of Keswick, after hearing an exposition of a passage concerning these ideas stated:

> "Has not my faith been *a seeking faith* when it ought to be *a resting faith*? And if so, why not exchange it for the latter? And I thought of the sufficiency of Jesus and said I will rest in Him—and I did rest in Him" (Pollock 7 *emphasis mine*).

This type of experience might be called the classic "Keswick experience." It also highlights the central theme of basic Keswick teaching: *the exchanged life*. The teachings of the convention have also been described as the *faith-rest life*. To state it simply, we are called to exchange our life of struggle and defeat with the victorious life of Christ. This life is available to any believer who is able to "let go" of their old life and "let God" take control.

The Secret of Victorious Living

Keswick, like Wesleyanism, has been accused of teaching that a believer can reach a state where he or she does not sin. Yet most in this tradition would see this as a misunderstanding of *how sin is defined* within the movement and also what "able not to sin" means. It is intrinsic to the Keswick message that the consecrated believer can move into a time in which the Holy Spirit empowers them to live victoriously over the power of sin and temptation. This, however, is not to be seen as *perfectionism*. The victorious believer is one who desires to live by the will of God and by the power of the Holy Spirit and therefore able to resist the temptation to *known sin*.

Keswick defines sin as having at least two expressions: 1) a *deliberate violation* of the known will of God, and 2) *unwittingly* (unknowingly) falling short of the glory of God.

> "If sin is defined to include this falling short unwittingly, Keswick does not teach that a person ever in this life has the ability not to sin. Yet, since so much of the emphasis of "victory" centers in the very area of disposition, spokesmen have often given the impression that consistent victory is possible, not only over temptation to conscious, deliberate acts of sin, but also over falling short in unconscious attitudes as well. But the "official" teaching has consistently been that every believer in this life is left with the natural proclivity to sin and will do so without the countervailing influence of the Holy Spirit" (McQuilkin 157).

Keswick generally does not see the battle with sin in the believer's life in terms of a battle between the "old man" and "new man", but in terms of a struggle between the *old sin nature* and the *new nature which is empowered by the indwelling Holy Spirit*. If a believer struggles with temptation and sin resulting in failure, he or she simply has not come to a "resting faith" in the power of God available to them. As long as there is a struggle with temptation and sin, the believer is not living in harmony with The Spirit or "in fellowship with God." This unbroken fellowship should be the ordinary experience of every believer.

Sanctification is seen as the process of removing or deterring the power of sin in the believer's life. The first act of sanctification is defined as *positional*. This positional sanctification is based in the finished work of Christ in which the believer is forgiven, justified, and regenerated. The second stage of sanctification is called *experiential sanctification*. Here, the believer is called to a life of holiness by the Spirit empowered removal of sinful attitudes and actions.

In order to walk in this victorious life, the believer must "commit all of oneself unconditionally to the person of God, who is revealed in the Bible and witnessed to by the Holy Spirit (1 Corinthians 2:14; Romans 10:17)" (McQuilkin, 169). This is the Keswick definition of *faith*. Yet this faith must be exercised on more than just the intellectual level. It must also be lived in *a life of obedience* to the known will of God.

Those who neglect the means of knowing God's will through study and meditation of Scripture, prayer, and active church involvement or who fall into a pattern of disobedience, may lapse into *passive drift*— what others call *backsliding*. This is a severe spiritual state, destructive to the believer's relationship with God. McQuilkin states,

> "Passive drift will distance a person from God just as surely as active rebellion, though it may take longer and prove more difficult to identify. Because the relationship is not easily recognized, especially by the person experiencing it, this condition is more dangerous than that of conscious rebellion. The original covenant relation with God has been violated, and the person can no longer experience the normal, Spirit-empowered life God promises. I believe that this passive drift into a condition of disobedience is the most common reason for failure in the Christian life" (McQuilkin 164).

The believer who is living a consecrated life of *unconditional surrender* to God through faith will possess an inner tranquility, Christ-like behavior, correct doctrinal confession, and an unwavering assurance of salvation. These tokens are viewed as the "evidences" of a true faith in the proper object, God. The most important evidence of true faith, however, is "unqualified commitment to doing the will of God" (McQuilkin 181). This type of obedience does not assure the quality or maturity of faith, but it does give evidence that faith is present.

Outward disobedience, on the other hand, gives evidence that a person has not surrendered completely to God, and the only solution is *complete surrender*. If continual "victory" is not evidenced in someone's life, two problems could be the cause: 1) they are a true Christian in *passive drift*, or 2) the person is *not saved at all*. A Christian who spends too much time in *passive drift* remains "out of fellowship with God" and increases the need for a more intense re-surrender to the power of the Spirit. The person who is not saved at all needs Jesus.

Signs and Means of the Spiritual Life

The Spirit-filled believer exhibits signs of growth both in the *inner mind* and *outward behavior*. The believer is encouraged to participate in the means that God uses to cause this growth. The primary factors that bring growth are:

1. **Scripture**: The Bible reveals God's will for the victorious life.

2. **Prayer**: Exhibits companionship with God and is the means of victory in temptation.

3. **Church Participation**: The ordinances, teaching, fellowship, discipline, and worship of the church are all necessary for continued growth.

4. **Suffering**: "God's greatest shortcut to spiritual growth." The way the believer responds to God's provision for suffering (trust that he has allowed it for the believer's benefit) helps the believer to become more like the "Suffering Servant" (McQuilkin 181).

McQuilkin summarizes the Keswick position this way:

"God Himself is the key to successful Christian living, and both He and His resources are available only to the person of faith. By faith alone we enter and maintain a personal relationship that releases an unending flow of grace. This biblical faith is both choice and attitude. The choice is to obey; and obedience begins with repentance, continues in a yielded spirit, and proves itself in aggressive participation in using the means of grace and in eager affirmative action to be all that God intends. The attitude is childlike trust, relying with loving confidence on Him alone" (McQuilkin 171).

Keswick spirituality has been one of *the* major influences on American Christianity. It has been popularized in the 20th Century by the writings of Lewis Sperry Chafer—*He That Is Spiritual,* Jack R. Taylor—*The Key to Triumphant Living,* Watchman Nee—*The Normal Christian Life* as well as those of A. W. Tozer, Major Ian Thomas, R. A. Torrey, F. B. Meyer, A. B. Simpson, and Charles Trumbill.

There has also been a unique vocabulary developed out of this tradition. Phrases such as, "the battle is not ours, it is the Lord's", "victory always, everywhere", "I did it in the flesh", "let go and let God", "die to self and live to Christ", "confession of every known sin", "I have a check in my spirit about that", "the Lord led me to do this", "I felt in my spirit the Lord telling me to...", "seeking the Lord's will" are all associated with Keswick spirituality (Houghton 16).

In 1946 Stephen Olford introduced Billy Graham to the Keswick convention, which Graham later said was like a second blessing to him. The teachings of Keswick can be traced to the founding of Dallas Theological Seminary. It is closely associated with the Bible Church/Nondenominational movement and laid the foundation for the theology of Bill Bright and Campus Crusade for Christ. The Keswick Convention is still held annually and is attended by men and women from a diverse range of denominations and traditions.

Visualizing Modern Spirituality

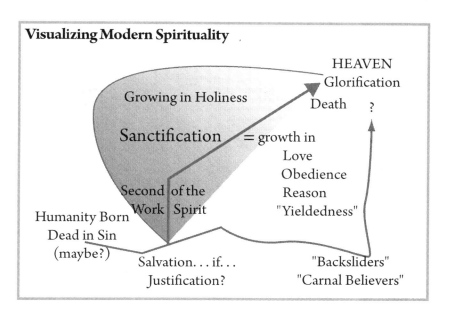

In The Background:
From PreModernity to PostModernity

As already stated, culture is a powerful influence in the shaping of theology. The mindsets and values of people are largely shaped by the "spirit of the times" (*zeitgeist*). If we do not understand how culture has influenced and is influencing the shape of human thought we will be blind to the effects it is having upon us in the present.

At the end of the 20th Century and the beginning of the 21st, one prevailing cultural "spirit" that must be addressed by Christianity is that of *hopelessness*. Western culture is now plagued by the belief that life is not getting better, nor is there any relief in sight. For many, life has become *meaningless*. There is no more graphic representation of this reality than in the rash of high-school shootings that took place in the late 1990s. *There is nothing more dangerous than a person without hope.*

As we study the diversity of Christian tradition and the spirituality that grows from it, we must also consider this important issue and try to discover not only why this has happened, but also how it should be addressed by the practice of our Christian beliefs and commitments.

Throughout human history (particularly Western history) there have been several key events that have led to major paradigm shifts.[43] In the area of religion, Jesus and His Apostles began a major paradigm shift resulting in Christianity becoming a major world religion. In secular history we could point to several key events of the last 2000 years that have shaped the trajectory of history. The Reformation (Martin Luther), the advent of "modern sciences", the invention of the printing press, the car, the airplane and micro-chip have all led to major paradigm shifts. Since the Birth of Christ, we could view history in terms of

---

43 A "paradigm shift" may be generally described as a major change in the way a people group views the world because of some person or event that impacts history in such a way that makes "looking at the world in the same old way" an impossibility.

three major eras based on significant paradigm shifts: the PreModern Era, the Modern Era, and the PostModern Era.

The PreModern Era

This era technically lasts from the classical era (ca. 500BC) until the time of The Renaissance in Southern Europe which culminates in The Enlightenment of the 18th Century. In this world our ancestors believed that life was influenced by spiritual forces (devils, demons, spirits, angels, etc.) which were beyond the perception of the five senses. The world was an "enchanted world." Sicknesses were not caused by bacteria or viruses (they had not been discovered yet) but by some "evil spirit" or, worse still, the anger of an offended deity. Most of the population in this era was illiterate.[44] There were no means of "mass-media" communication as any book or document had to be produced by hand and were, therefore, very expensive and accessible to a privileged few.

The world was viewed a large (flat) space with limits. Most dared not venture too far from the place of their birth—after all, it was possible sail right off the face of the Earth as Christopher Columbus was warned. Security and protection in the world came from keeping things close to "kith and kin." There were no banks in the modern sense of the word, at least not for the common man, and the idea of acquiring wealth was left only for kings and popes.

The idea of the "Divine Right of Kings" was also widely accepted. In this worldview, worldly rulers were established by God and to oppose the king was to oppose God himself (however He was defined).[45] In the West this idea led to the oppression of the feudal land systems and also to the subjugation of the masses under Roman Christendom. The king was crowned by Pope the human representative of God Himself.

---

44 Several studies have shown that in the Middle East of the First Century as much as 80-90% of the population could not read or write.

45 This view is seen clearly in ancient cultures such as Egypt and even Israel. Pharaoh was viewed to be a "son of the Gods" who was invested with all their authority. In a like manner the Psalms of David to his kingship in terms of his relationship to God as a "son."

Separation of Church and State was unheard of; the Church was the State.

Life was much simpler and less complicated than it is now. The only priority that most of the ancients had was staying alive. The PreModerns were not bogged by the trivialities that plague life today. The particulars of life were given cohesion by family, society, and faith. It was more important to belong to the community than to be an individual. Only the heretics and the false prophets stood out from the crowd.

The Modern Era

The ideas of the PreModern world came under severe attack in the Modern Era. Both the best and worst ideas of this era were fueled and propagated on a scale previously unavailable by the invention of the *printing press* by Johannes Guttenberg in the 15th Century. Now the ability to put printed material in the hands of the common man ushered in a new age of literacy, creativity, and "mass communication." The learning institutions of the so called "dark ages" flowered into the Universities, some of which exist to this day.

The education of the common man and the rediscovery of *classical ideals* of ancient Greece and Rome led to *The Renaissance* in southern Europe. Art, music, literature, and science began to develop into the modern forms that we are most familiar with in the present. What was birthed in The Renaissance grew to maturity in *The Enlightenment* which took place in Europe beginning in the mid 1600's and ending in 1789 with the French Revolution.

During this time, the West saw the development of all the great sciences that have become the foundation of our society. Newton, Galileo, Copernicus, and many others ushered in a scientific revolution which gave us calculus, modern physics and paved the way for the great social sciences of the 19th and 20th centuries—sociology, psychology, and anthropology. It was a period marked by radical social, political, scientific, and industrial upheavals.

The causes and catalysts for The Enlightenment are too complex to review in this study. For our purposes we can simply say that at the heart of this major upheaval was a *rejection of the traditional authoritarian views of the world* (particularly the Roman Catholic) and *an acceptance of human reason and ability as the locus of authority*. God would be exiled and humanity itself would become the new sovereign.

The most significant development during this era scientifically (and spiritually) is that of Darwinism. Based on Charles Darwin's studies and the publication *The Origin of Species by Means of Natural Selection, or The Preservation of Favoured Races in the Struggle for Life*, science began to embrace the idea that humanity was not the creation of God, but the latest stage in animal *evolution* on the planet. Man was more akin to the monkey than he was to God.

But also notice very carefully the second line of the title of Darwin's original publication—*The Preservation of* **Favoured** *Races in the Struggle for Life*. If evolution does exist within humanity, then some "races" of must be more advanced than others. This "scientific fact" became the foundation for the genocidal policies of the totalitarian 20th Century regimes: Nazism in Germany, Fascism in Italy, Communism in Eastern Europe and Russia, the dictatorships in Asia.

Human reason was placed on the pedestal of praise and glory during this era. Though many of the fathers of the modern sciences were themselves pious men of Christian faith, their works unfortunately allowed the infidels to call for an end to the irrelevant belief in God or Personal Creator. If the existence of the universe can be explained by science and the determinacy of mere chance, then why do we need Him?

But even Darwin himself had a "horrid doubt" that humanity could think properly about anything at all, especially if our minds are still essentially monkey minds:

> "But then with me the horrid doubt always arises whether the convictions of man's mind, which has been developed from the mind of the lower animals, are of any value or at all trustworthy. Would any one trust in the convictions of a monkey's mind, if there

are any convictions in such a mind?" (Charles Darwin letter to William Graham, July 3, 1881)

This science based shift of thinking led to viewing the world and universe as a great machine and as a result the world became mechanized. The modern era may in a very real sense be viewed as the Era of the Machines, with man as their sovereign creator.

The machines opened the door for the *industrial age*. Mass production took the creation of the products needed for life out of the hands of the trade guilds of earlier times and assigned them to the de-humanized environment of the *factory*. The progress of industry stripped away from the craftsman and artisan the satisfaction of personal accomplishment and relegated their talents to the periphery of life.

This effect, however, was redefined as the freeing of the individual from menial tasks so that *he*[46] could be free to become a better person pursuing the "better life." The idea of a "fallen humanity" was replaced with the idea that humanity was simply at a stage of its evolution when it had not yet matured to its full potential. The individual was not *inherently bad* or *evil* and could therefore *perfect* himself through the pursuit of "goodness" or morality or any other endeavor that allowed him to achieve "all that he could be." Until this point in history, humanity had not existed in the proper context so that human goodness could flower to its full potential. The "Renaissance Man" would become the new hero; a man perfectly balanced through the application of logic and emotion learned through the *liberal arts* (art, science, literature, music).

With the promise of the "good life" also came the promise of *progress*. Technology and the machines would make it possible for life to become less complicated and the advances of this golden age would ultimately produce air-conditioning, a longer lasting light bulb, and the microwave oven. This science-driven, progressive world removed the need for "spiritual" realities. *Secularism*, the stripping away of all

---

46 I have used "he" in this context purposefully. These ideals were meant only for men. Women were to be kept and tolerated for the birthing of children and maintaining the household (or for the personal pleasure of men).

symbols and practice of religion, may best describe the spiritual goals and effects of modernism.

Scientism[47], which is a central component of the Modern Worldview, excluded all other sources and methods of knowledge that were not naturalistic in nature. It also rejected and displaced the older Worldviews, particularly that generated from The Bible. The Scientists knows there are unseen forces but has new names for them: quarks, dark matter, etc. There are mysteries, but it is only a matter of time before our scientists are able to figure them out. Scientism as the new prevailing secular religion has not, however, given us a story satisfying enough to find transcendent meaning and purpose.[48] Neil Postman comments,

> "...in the end, science does not provide the answers most of us require. Its story of our origins and of our end is, to say the least, unsatisfactory. To the question, "How did it all begin?", science answers, "Probably by an accident." To the question, "How will it all end?", science answers, "Probably by an accident." And to many people, the accidental life is not worth living" ("Science and the Story We Need").

If we follow the story told by naturalism and scientism, we find ourselves cut off from the meaning of our past without a clear hope for the future and therefore abandoned to the isolation of the present. The individual is lost, having no vision beyond what is happening now. William B. Provine sums up this Modernist view succinctly:

---

47 "Scientism is belief in the universal applicability of the scientific method and approach, and the view that empirical science constitutes the most "authoritative" worldview or the most valuable part of human learning—to the exclusion of other viewpoints" (Wikipedia).

48 Even though many would take issue with the assertion that scientism is a religion, the facts are obvious. Science tells its own story (meta-narrative) about the origins of human life. It has its own priesthood (the scientists) that propagates its doctrines. It censors all those who do not agree with the accepted teachings (heretics). It reveres and honors its own set of saints who established its tradition. And most importantly, it requires faith to accept some of its tenets which have not been proved.

"Let me summarize my views on what modern evolutionary biology tells us loud and clear, and I must say that these are basically Darwin's views. There are no gods, no purposeful forces of any kind, no life after death. When I die, I am absolutely certain that I am going to be completely dead. That's just all—that's gonna be the end of me. There is no ultimate foundation for ethics, no ultimate meaning in life, and no free will for humans, either."[49]

If we think about the effects of the Enlightenment and modernity in purely materialistic standards, it has its successes. Many of the modern advances have made life in The West better, or at the very least, easier. Spiritually, the Enlightenment has proved to be *a miserable disaster*.

The PostModern Era

With such promise, how is it that the 20th Century became the stage for some of the most evil and violent acts of humanity ever? Our times are marked by cynicism and despair which give birth to hopelessness. How did we get here?

The PostModern World has evolved out of the failed promises of Modernity. Even though the modern western world has made life incredibly comfortable for most,[50] the secularized culture has failed to provide the individual with answers about the *ultimate meaning* of life. Without a way to answer the questions of meaning and purpose, many find it difficult, if not impossible, to attain any level of *spiritual* satisfaction. Modernity has given us more "stuff" but most of that "stuff" does little to move us beyond self-interest, much less to the redemptive and

49 Provine, W.B., *Darwinism*: *Science or Naturalistic Philosophy? The Debate at Stanford University*, William B. Provine and Phillip E. Johnson, videorecording © 1994 Regents of the University of California.

50 One of the most glaring problems facing the West is that of the homeless. Our big cities—the very symbols of the progress of modernity—are still filled with the hungry and the homeless despite the dream of science and technology being able to solve these problems. Although a very complex issue, at the root of this problem still lies the treachery and foolishness of the unredeemed human heart: some people will never help even if the have the power, resources and opportunity to do so (greed) and others cannot be helped due to a number of various mental infirmities (pride, ignorance, mental dysfunction, etc.)

transformative virtues of hope, faith, love, self-sacrifice, and service to others.

The *individualism* of the Modern period collapsed into the *collectivism* that defined much of the 20th Century. The rise of Socialism, Fascism, Nazism, and Communism put an end to the pipe-dreams of *liberty* for all mankind that was part of the great hope of the modern experiment. Man is not autonomous as the moderns had hoped, instead he has become one more tiny wheel in The Machine.

World War I called into question the modernist hope in the upward progress of humanity. The belief in the *inherent goodness of humanity* was incinerated in the ovens of the concentration camps in Eastern Europe during World War II. The possibility of human perfectibility gave way to war, racism, and unspeakable *atrocity*. The same technology that paved the way for the "better life" envisioned by the moderns also made possible the weapons of mass destruction. The Golden Age gave way to the Nuclear Age.

Hope for the future turned to despair. Many of the steps that the moderns had taken to secularize the world and strip all religion out of human experience only opened the doors for the extreme forms of *alienation* and *disenchantment* that characterize life at the end of the 20th Century. The family has been replaced by the "broken home," and personal contact has been superseded by all "e-forms" of interaction. If humans were truly created to exist in relationship as the Bible affirms, the postmodern era has done its best to destroy this possibility. Our mechanized, digitized world created by science is one in which the human spirit has been left homeless.

> "Of particular relevance for postmodern spirituality is concern for spiritual experience and human connectedness, disillusionment with material possessions, and distrust of the institutional church" (Bruce Demarest, *Four Views on Christian Spirituality*, 13).

We often find ourselves estranged from our families, drowning in our culture, unsatisfied by our jobs—all realities which should give us a sense of identity, belonging, and purpose. Without faith in something larger than ourselves to anchor us, we are adrift in the sea of *whatever*.

Living a life of significance shared with others for the benefit of all has been replaced by living life pursuing the "American dream" of acquiring success and wealth. This in turn has put a great strain on all forms of relationship. Since we have forgotten how to live with other humans, we pour more of our time and energy into jobs which leads to more alienation at home, among friends, etc. We no longer have "vocations"—meaningful and skillful work done in the good service of the community. Now we all have jobs in which toil to make an increasingly smaller number of people wealthy.

The *personnel* office has been replaced by *human resources*. In Post-Modern times, the individual as a resource is used up by the corporation, the organization, or some other collective which will discard the broken body when it has finally stripped it of all value and usefulness. *Resistance is futile, you will be assimilated.*

In postmodern times, *hope has died*. If there is no greater meaning in life beyond that which humanity can produce, then all life is meaningless. Try as they might, the moderns never gave an adequate substitute for the Creator they "killed." Science has failed to give an adequate explanation of life in a way that gives it significance and meaning. If humanity is only the product of *impersonal* chance, natural selection and evolution then why should we hope to find meaningful, personal answers to anything? When the universe is through with us, we will be replaced or maybe just annihilated. And in the impersonal universe there will be no one who will care.

Since Modernism killed all traditional means of access to *transcendent truth*, the postmodern person is left to despair, pondering whether or not there is even such a thing as truth. Many, like Fox Mulder, have some vague hope that "the truth is out there," but it is very doubtful that they will ever find it. The idea of a meta-narrative—a larger story, THE Story that makes sense of life on earth by answering the questions of our origin, purpose and destiny—has been summarily dismissed.

Because there is no Larger Story that makes all the smaller stories cohere and make sense, life has become senseless. We are born, we live, we die—that's it.

The Church, who used to give answers to these questions, has been side-lined due to out own internal squabbles and our miserable track record of handling "worldly power." No one has ever really forgiven the Roman church for the Middle Ages. Because Christians themselves often don't live out the reality of The Story they proclaim, why should anyone else take them seriously.

When the Foundations are Destroyed

Maybe the Bible spoke better than what the Moderns could now when the Psalmist asked,

> When the Foundations are destroyed,
> what can the Righteous do? (Psalm 11:3)

It is important to understand how these (mostly negative) trends in culture have shaped not only the Christian pursuit of spirituality, but also how they have affected the view of spiritual life of the secular community. In the PreModern era, the cultures of Greece and Rome provided a philosophical foundation of logic that gave great stability to the societies they ruled. However, with the Christian upheaval of Western history in the 4th-6th Centuries followed by the reign of the Roman church over the secular and the sacred, many of these "classical" ideals were forgotten or purposely censured. The Roman Imperial Captivity of Christianity was a reign of the "terror of God." If the institutional church could determine who would go to Heaven and who would be consigned to Hell, then all matters of this life were under its control as well. He who has the "keys of the Kingdom" controls the universe.

In the 14th and 15th centuries a return to classical ideals by radical opponents of the Roman church led to the birth of the Modern era. However, as we have just seen, these modern ideals paved the way for the utter despair and hopelessness of the 20th Century. As we will see, these trends also affected the development of several key spiritual movements within Christianity. *In some sense, the pursuit of spirituality is the pursuit of hope. When hope dies, so does the pursuit of the spiritual.*

Here at the end of this very bleak section, we have to remember that no matter how dark human history gets, the Bible affirms that in the end Father-God will accomplish His purposes in Christ through the Holy Spirit. In the very beginning, God takes the "stuff" of earth that was "formless and void" and by His power and wisdom shapes it and fills it into something "very good." At the end of Genesis, Joseph is sold into slavery by his brothers, a wicked act for sure, but this is the very thing that God uses for good, to save and preserve the family of Abraham (see Genesis 50:20).

Jesus was sent by the Father to be hated, despised, beaten, tortured, and ultimately killed by the very people He was sent to save. Yet in this, the most evil act humanity has ever committed, Father-God accomplished His plans for salvation, the final defeat of evil, and the guarantee of a New Creation. Throughout all history, what mankind has done as evil, the Lord-God—in His inscrutable wisdom and power—has purposed for good. This great, transcendent truth is the only basis for hope that any of us can have.

Hope in Progress and the Spirit of the Times

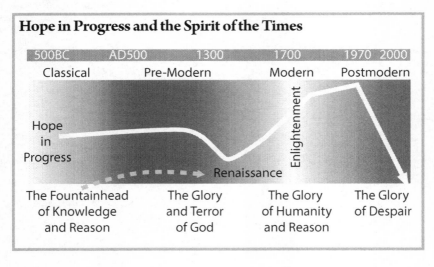

MOVEMENTS IN THE 20TH CENTURY

Christian spirituality in the 20th Century was largely shaped by two forces: the struggle *within* Christianity between *liberals* and *conservatives*, and the struggle with the secular forces on the *outside*. With the spread of "higher critical methods" in the 19th Century, the traditional and fundamental doctrines of Christianity were shaken to the core by the charge that the Bible is only a hodge-podge collection of anachronistic, human-edited materials and not the actual revelation of a transcendent, personal God.

With the rise of Darwinism and the resulting avalanche of atheistic emphases in the scientific community, Christianity was blind-sided with the charge that not only is the Bible entirely misunderstood (as the liberals within Christianity affirmed), but it is also an implausible explanation for life on Earth. In this sense, Christian spirituality in the 20th Century developed in a militant atmosphere fighting for the truth and its survival. Yet just as culture in general, Christianity in the West turned to the *experience of the individual* and the *power of democratic capitalism* as the dominant influences for spirituality.

Two major *philosophical shifts* can be seen as the driving force behind movements that have shaped spirituality in this century. First, both *tradition* and *reason* have been denounced as reliable and authoritative sources for truth. Generally speaking, if tradition is to be a guide to THE Truth, then which one is right—Christian, Hindu, Muslim? Or more to the point, within Christianity, who is right?—the Methodists, the Baptists, the Presbyterians? If truth is absolute, then everyone cannot claim that their particular tradition contains *all truth* especially when everyone else says otherwise. What is more, *reason*—the ability to *think* about truth—has been called into question. The Enlightenment ideal put reason on the pedestal of human achievement. Through his reason, man would be able to produce great technology and usher in a 'golden age' where there will be no hunger, no diseases, etc. Yet the question boils down to this:"If humanity is progressing so much technologically, why is life not getting better?" Two World Wars in the 20th Century did not help answer the question.

The second major shift occurred with the rise of the *individual* being the sole source of truth and authority. This is at the root of the Postmodern understanding of life. Since all other forms of authority —reason, tradition, religion, etc.—have failed, then the experience of the individual must be the only "truth." *Carpe Diem* (seize the day) becomes the motto of the intellectual community, whereas "Just do it!" better serves the tastes of a general public fattened by a constant diet of mass marketing, preaching the new gospel of a kinder, gentler god— *me and my freedom of choice.*

As Christianity develops in this century, two opposing forces battle for supremacy. On the right, hard-core *conservatives* call for a return to the Bible (as they interpret it) as the sole arbiter of truth for life. On the left, the *liberals* embrace culture as a valid interpreter and tool for redefining the core truths of Christianity and their application. Now at the in the second decade of the 21st Century it is pretty clear who won.

By the 1990s, the Mega-church mind-set ruled as the quest for 'church growth' became the new motivating force for a new breed of minister trained in the *business* of Christianity. The day of the "Rock-Star Pastor" finally arrived and we have all become fans.

By the end of the 20th Century, The Bible had been translated into almost every major human language with at least 100 different versions in English alone. Yet with all these resources available, *basic Biblical literacy is at an all time low*. The Bible is everywhere, but no one seems to know what it says or what it means. And in the Western world even fewer really care. Life is good, why get too serious, dude?

Pentecostalism

The term Pentecostal comes from the Feast of Pentecost, the Greek name for the Jewish Feast of Weeks. For Christians, this event commemorates the descent of the Holy Spirit upon the first disciples, recorded in Acts 2.

The modern Pentecostal movement was catalyzed at Bethel Bible College in Topeka Kansas in 1900. The founder, Charles Parham, established the school on a faith basis, charging no tuition. He invited anyone who was willing to leave all, sell what they had, give away the proceeds, and come to the school for study and prayer. Around 40 people came. Parham, a former Methodist who had become disenchanted with all denominationalism, used The Bible only as a textbook and proclaimed the Holy Spirit to be the only true teacher, with Parham himself as His mouthpiece.

By the end of 1900, Parham had taught that there had to be a deeper experience with God, although he did not yet point the students to speaking in tongues or other signs. Parham had heard of this phenomena while visiting and studying various other "later day" restorationist movements. Although the accounts vary as to what actually happened, at the end of the term in December 1900, Parham took a few days off and the students continued to pray and study. At a student led worship service on January 1, 1901 Agnes Ozman asked to be prayed over to receive a fuller experience of the Holy Spirit. Immediately after the prayer, she began to speak in "tongues" (another language not known to the speaker).

This event solidified basic Pentecostal teaching that "speaking in tongues" is the "initial outward evidence that a person has been baptized in the Holy Spirit as an empowering experience for Christian Service" (Horton 105). This early beginning reached a peak in the ministry of W. J. Seymour in the church at 312 Azusa Street in Los Angeles.

At Azusa, people from all cultural and ethnic backgrounds gathered for "full praise and worship" of Jesus. The work at this church was heavily influenced by the Wesleyan holiness background which, by that time, came to believe that a *preparatory sanctification experience* was necessary for receiving the baptism *of* the Holy Spirit. Sanctification became viewed as a "second definite work of grace" cleansing believers from sin, making them a fit vessel for the Holy Spirit to fill.

A House Divided

Like all the other traditions we have reviewed, the Pentecostal movement has many different "flavors." A significant rift was introduced in this tradition in 1910 when William H. Durham began to preach what he called the "finished work of Calvary." Contrary to the earlier holiness preaching, Durham taught that justifying faith also made the believer one with Christ and therefore *complete* in Him. The new believer truly becomes a "new creature" by faith and *needs no other work of grace for sanctification*. The Spirit provides all that is necessary and the believer responds by abiding in Christ, walking by the Spirit, and avoiding sin. Like other strands of reformed teaching, the sinful nature has been crucified with Christ but not removed. By living a life of faith, the believer can live free of the power of sin. If sin is present, the believer is out of fellowship with Christ and simply needs to turn back to Him, turning away from the inclinations of the sinful nature.

The division that was introduced by Durham's teaching exists to this day. The *Holiness Pentecostal* movement still holds to a "crisis experience of sanctification as a *second* definite work of the Holy Spirit." Those who follow Durham's teaching, such as the Assemblies of God, generally see "faith and the cleansing of the blood of Christ as the only prerequisite for baptism in the Spirit" (Horton 109).

In the Assemblies of God, another split was caused over the nature of The Trinity. Some within this movement took the non-Wesleyan "finished work of Calvary" teaching to an extreme which led to the conclusion that Jesus was the full expression of the *name* of God. Basing these conclusions on what they found in Acts, this group claimed that *Jesus* is *the* name of the Father, Son and Holy Spirit in the baptismal formula of Matthew 28:19. The Trinity is understood *modalistically* with Jesus being the only "person" in the Godhead. This new Pentecostal *unitarianism* became what is now known as the "Oneness" or "Jesus Only" movement. The only true baptism was one done in Jesus' name alone; all who had been baptized in the name of the "Father, Son and Holy Ghost" would have to be re-baptized in Jesus' name alone. Those within the Assemblies who disagreed with the position (Trinitarian Pentecostals) soon adopted a sixteen point Statement of *Fundamental Truths* which denounced this doctrine.

This *Statement of Fundamental Truths*, however, raised another point of contention within the non-Oneness camp. Point 9 of the statement called the believer to a life of holiness, based on 1 Peter 1:16-17 (Be holy, for I am holy…), and *entire sanctification*. Since no definition of *entire sanctification* was given, many felt that some would confuse the idea with the earlier Wesleyan Pentecostal Holiness "second work of Grace" and therefore called for the point to be emended. In the revised point, the term *entire sanctification* was removed and the ideas of *positional* and *progressive* sanctification were explained.

Defining Sanctification

Through the Cross and the merit of Christ's blood, the believer has *positional* sanctification. This is based on the teaching of Christ's "finished work on Calvary." The *holiness* of the believer is secured by Christ's work alone in justification by faith. There is, however, a *progressive* aspect to sanctification. Since a *life of holiness* (demonstrated in behavior and attitude) is necessary, the believer must "cooperate with the work of God" in his or her life to produce sanctification.

Paul teaches in Colossians 3:5-10 that the believer is to "put to death…whatever belongs to your earthly nature…" This does not mean "that the whole responsibility for progressive sanctification is put on the believer. *We have our part, but God also has His part*" (Horton 117 *emphasis mine*).

Although there has been some hesitancy for those in the more conservative line of the Pentecostal tradition to use the term "entire sanctification," the idea is still present some preaching and teaching. Horton argues that the term may now be used in three different senses: 1) for believers who live "up to the light that they have," (i.e. *do the best they can* at their stage of maturity), 2) a *relative perfection* in which the believer is fully submitting to the work of the Holy Spirit with the end result being full sanctification (in Heaven), or 3) *glorification*—the state into which the believer will be transformed at Christ's second coming. Most of the Assemblies of God hold to this last position.

Although each of these views contains parts of the other, the thing to note is that in recent times the idea of entire sanctification *has not been taught as sinless perfection*, which is to say that the believer reaches a state in which they are *not able to sin*. Yet more in line with John Wesley's theology (not to be confused with the Wesleyanism that developed later), that the believer grows in sanctification, becomes more and more *able not to sin*.[51] By the work of the Holy Spirit the believer is able to have victory over temptation to sin.

Cooperating With the Spirit

The Holy Spirit is seen as the agent of both the positional and progressive aspect of sanctification. This agency is accomplished not by an infallible work of the Spirit, but as a cooperative effort between the Spirit and the believer:

> "The Holy Spirit through whom we have sanctification, or consecration…, also enables us to cooperate with this work by purifying our souls in obedience to the truth, resulting in a sincere brotherly love… The work of the Spirit in sanctification thus brings growth in grace and brings about the development of the fruit of the Spirit" (Horton 119).

The idea that the believer must "cooperate" in this work is highly important for the Pentecostal view. Basically, this means an obedience

---

51 This whole argument is somewhat related to the "impeccability of Christ" debate. Was Christ *non posse peccare* "not able to sin," or was he simply *posse non peccare* "able not to sin"? The wording is very important. Since the Bible is specifically silent on both accounts, the debate will continue.

to the truth of the Bible. This obedience is exercised in study of the Word which informs the believer how to live in right relationship with God and man, as well as how to avoid things that would cripple the pursuit of holiness.[52] Yet there remains some ambiguity as to just how much the believer is expected to "cooperate." Even though the Holy Spirit is affirmed to be solely responsible for the work of sanctification, the believer is still given some responsibility—it is not an automatic, mechanized process:

> "First, there must be a true reliance on the Spirit to make one holy; misconceptions of the process of sanctification must be renounced. Some Christians conduct themselves as though they believe holiness to be the inevitable result of simply professing Christ long enough... Other Christians apparently believe that sanctification is achieved by an increasing effort to become godly through one's own strength. But just as growth in a plant is the result of life, not effort, so holiness is the result of an indwelling, living Holy Spirit. Still another misconception about sanctification is that the Christian makes the effort and then asks God to bless it. But the Holy Spirit must do the whole work, or none of it; He will not share the work with man. Without taking Christ's righteousness and the Spirit's application of it, man will find both wind and tide opposed to him" (Horton 127-28).

Baptism in the Spirit

One of the key theological distinctions of Pentecostal doctrine concerns the Baptism of the Holy Spirit. Horton states that,

> "...there is a distinction between the baptism *by* the Spirit [1 Corinthians 12:3], which incorporates believers into the body of Christ, and the baptism *in* the Spirit, in which Christ is the Baptizer

---

52   One of the most extreme applications of this view is present in the rural pentecostal "snake handling" communities in the Appalachian region of the US. Taking the words of Mark 16:17-18 literally (*part of the so called "longer ending" of Mark which most scholars agree was a later scribal addition not part of the original Gospel*), this group "takes up serpents," handling deadly, venomous snakes and drinks poison to show the power of their faith. If someone is bitten and dies, (as many have) it is because the individual did not have enough faith.

and where the purpose is to empower the believer through the filling of the Spirit (Luke 24:49; Acts 1:8; 2:4)" (Horton 130).

In other words, Pentecostals teach that there is a secondary baptizing and filling of the Spirit *distinct* from the baptism that occurs at the moment of justification, the beginning of regeneration. The "overflowing fullness" of the Holy Spirit may then give the believer a deeper reverence for God, a more active love for Christ or His word, the ability to evangelize more powerfully, the ability to work supernatural signs, etc.

This one aspect of Pentecostal theology has been one of the most hotly debated issues by those both within and outside the tradition. Some of the more radical Pentecostal groups have claimed that those who do not receive this second baptism of the Spirit, as witnessed by speaking in tongues, are not truly saved. However, as Horton points out, in at least one form of Pentecostalism, the baptism *in* the Holy Spirit is not primarily to make one more "saved" or holy, but to empower the believer for service:

> "…we believe that the chief object of our Christian life is not to purify ourselves. Growth in grace comes best as we are involved in service. We do not believe that the saint, or dedicated believer should spend every day in nothing but study, prayer, and devotion. Those things are important, but the holy, sanctified life involves much more. We can see an illustration in the holy vessels in the tabernacle. They could not be used for ordinary purposes. No one could take them into their kitchen and cook with them, nor could they take them to their dining table and eat from them. Yet it was not their separation from ordinary use that made them holy. They were not holy until they were taken into the tabernacle and actually used in the service of God. So we are saints, not merely because we are separated from sin and evil, but because we are separated to God, sanctified and anointed for the Master's use" (Horton 132).

Charismatics and Signs and Wonders

By the 1960's and 70's basic Pentecostal ideas had made their way into many mainstream denominations. This *Charismatic* movement placed a greater emphasis on the role of the Holy Spirit, particularly in the practice of the spiritual gifts, and the continuance of miracles in the present day.

By the 1980's another major development called the "Signs and Wonders" movement sprang out of Pentecostalism. Spearheaded by men like John Wimber and C. Peter Wagner,[53] this movement stressed that Christianity was not only to preach the Gospel, but also to show the power of the Gospel through healing and miraculous signs. Signs are defined in terms of anything from having an ecstatic vision, to physical healing, to "barking," or "laughing" in the Spirit.[54] Accepting most of the core Pentecostal beliefs, this movement focused on the experience of the believer and the affecting of miraculous works through the power of the Holy Spirit. This movement is best known through The Vineyard Assemblies and in Wimber's popular book, *Power Evangelism*.

In the theology of this movement, greater emphasis is given to *experiencing* the reality of God. John Wimber explains:

> "So God uses our experience to show us more fully what He teaches in Scripture, many times toppling or altering elements of our theology and worldview" (Wimber).

Experience, if I am interpreting Wimber's views correctly, is almost *equal in authority* to tradition or even the Written Word of Scripture. Whatever the case, it is clear from even a cursory scanning of Wimber's printed and recorded teachings that the *subjective experience of the individual* is more important in the pursuit of spirituality than the *objective*

---

53 This movement was closely associated with Fuller Theological Seminary where both Wimber and Wagner taught. Their class "MC510—Signs, Wonders and Church Growth" was a pivotal development of this movement. Men like Charles Kraft were significantly influenced by this teaching.

54 "Barking," or "laughing in the Spirit" is a fairly recent development (90's) but shows the extent to which the quest for the "miraculous" becomes the center of some forms of Pentecostal "worship."

acquisition of knowledge. God is inviting the believer to "experience" His power rather than define Him through logic and reason.

One of the unique aspects of this movement is the call for a "paradigm shift" in modern Christian thinking. Wimber, Wagner, and Charles Kraft have heavily criticized the "western mind set" that has dominated the interpretation of Scripture since the age of The Enlightenment. The "paradigm shift" these men are calling for is a shift toward seeing things from a more "middle-eastern subjective mindset." Wimber teaches, "We must remember always that the Bible was written in the Middle East, not with *rational assumption*, that we bring to it as we try to understand it, but with an *experiential assumption*" (Scott 19).

Wimber seems to be arguing that the Bible is not to be viewed as a book that can be known *objectively* through reason, but one that is to be viewed through the *subjective* lenses of experience. This might be akin to the old "head knowledge" vs. "heart knowledge" dichotomy—We should not so much try to understand God mentally, as we should seek to experience Him intimately. "God is bigger than His written Word," is a good summary of the of the way this movement applies the use of experience as a determining factor for theology.[55]

The Latter Rain

The Signs and Wonders movement is viewed within some circles of Pentecostalism as the final stage in the pouring out of the fullness of the Holy Spirit in the end times in the "latter rain" of blessing as spoken of by the prophets.[56] C. Peter Wagner described it as the "Third Wave" of Pentecostal progress. The "First Wave" began in 1901 at Bethel Bible

---

55   These are John Wimber's own words from Church Planting Seminar, Tapes I, II, III, IV, V, March 28, 1981.

56   Deut. 11:14 "that He will give the rain for your land in its season, the early and late rain, that you may gather in your grain and your new wine and your oil." Joel 2:23 "Be glad then, ye children of Zion, and rejoice in the Lord your God: for he hath given you the former rain moderately, and he will cause to come down for you the rain, the former rain, and the latter rain in the first month." Zechariah 10:1 "Ask ye of the Lord rain in the time of the latter rain; so the Lord shall make bright clouds, and give them showers of rain, to every one grass in the field."

college with the illumination that took place there and was followed by the "Second Wave" in which "speaking in tongues" gained widespread acceptance and paved the way for the more intense expression of the Spirit in the "Third Wave."

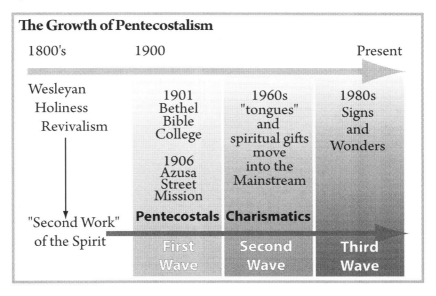

The Growth of Pentecostalism

1800's	1900		Present
Wesleyan Holiness Revivalism	1901 Bethel Bible College 1906 Azusa Street Mission	1960s "tongues" and spiritual gifts move into the Mainstream	1980s Signs and Wonders
"Second Work" of the Spirit	**Pentecostals**	**Charismatics**	
	First Wave	Second Wave	Third Wave

Pentecostalism is a powerful renewal movement akin to the other Restorationist movements within Protestant Christianity. It is also the catalyst for the modern Charismatic movement that has brought an emphasis back to the practice of the *spiritual gifts* in many of the traditional mainstream denominations. This Charismatic renewal touches almost every branch of Protestantism as well as Roman Catholicism.

There are around 700 pentecostal denominations worldwide and the movement continues to grow especially in the southern hemisphere. In recent years the tradition has gained a wide audience in large part due to "mass media appeal" through radio and television. The *Trinity Broadcasting Network* has grown to be a major force in the dissemination of Pentecostal ideals. Negatively, this tradition has been corrupted in the ministries of the Tel-evangelists.

Major Influence: Fundamentalism

Just prior to and immediately after World War I, a movement arose in the US to combat the negative influence that liberalism was having in academic Christianity. The goal of this movement was to reaffirm orthodox Protestant Christianity and to defend it against the attacks of liberal theology in general, German higher criticism in particular, along with Darwinism and any of the other "isms" set against Conservative Christianity. From 1910 to 1915 a series of twelve volumes called *The Fundamentals* was published outlining the "enemies of Christianity" and the key doctrines that one must affirm to be considered a Christian. The authors contributing to this publication came from a diverse background both denominationally and nationally.

Although, in recent times the idea of "fundamentalism" has been demonized as being stern and legalistic, this was not the original intention of the movement or its publications:

> "*The Fundamentals*, especially in the first seven or eight volumes, was an attempt to be broad and well-rounded, doctrinal as well as experiential, educational and intelligently apologetic, and tolerant and considerate of those they criticized. Their aim was to help equip Protestant workers in their ministries to understand the new situation in Christianity when alternatives to and departures from orthodoxy were both numerous and successful" (McIntyre).

Romanism, socialism, Mormonism, Eddyism, spiritualism, Darwinism, German higher criticism were all denounced as harmful influences which undermined the authority of the Bible, or more to the point, those teachings which called the very validity of the Bible into question. The Fundamentalist movement saw itself at war with these competing philosophies and the prize—the reality and validity of the idea of *objective truth*—would be the spoils of battle.

Yet the movement was not entirely polemic. It also called for the confession and affirmation of the traditional pillars of Christian truth such as the inerrancy and inspiration of the Bible, the virgin birth of

Jesus, the substitutionary atonement of Christ, the Resurrection, and the historicity of miracles—all doctrines which were being called into question by the liberal academic establishment.

These issues, as well as others, became the focus of divisive struggles within many denominations during this period. The affirmation or denial of what was delineated to be "orthodox" clearly drew the line in the sand for the opposing factions. Two of the greatest battles took place in the northern Presbyterian (led by J. Gresham Machen) and the northern Baptist denominations. The Southern Baptist denomination ascended to the top of the fundamentalist movement in the South. The great fundamentalist debate, however, was not argued within the Church, but in the courtroom over the teaching of Darwinism in public schools in the famous Scopes Trial of 1925.

By the 1940's and 50's, fundamentalism began to make claims on culture in general. A heavy emphasis on moralism sprung up in which smoking, drinking, theater going, movie watching, card-playing, and gambling were all denounced. By the 1960's and 70's the tolerance that had been evidenced in the early movement had all but disappeared. This may be due in some part to the rise of modern Evangelicalism *out* of Fundamentalism.

Whereas the new Evangelicals affirmed many of the traditional doctrines, it took a more relaxed approach toward culturally centered issues.

> "…fundamentalists believed they differed from evangelicals… by being more faithful to Bible-believing Christianity, more militant against church apostasy, communism, and personal evils, less ready to cater to social and intellectual respectability. They tended to oppose evangelist Billy Graham, not to read *Christianity Today,* and not to support Wheaton College or Fuller Theological Seminary. Instead they favored their own evangelists, radio preachers, newspapers, and schools" (McIntyre).

In the present, it is often hard to distinguish between Fundamentalism and Evangelicalism since they both stand for many of the same ideas. Yet there remains a certain *militancy* with many Fundamentalists that is not present in other Evangelical leaders.

Another distinguishing mark of modern Fundamentalism is that it tends to view America as a type of "promised land" that is falling into the clutches of secular humanism and being polluted by non-biblical morality, sexual perversions, socialism, communism, and any other group or force that stands contrary to God's Truth. There is a tendency to see the United States as being a country founded on Christian ideals yet now straying from them. Therefore, at least one of the goals of fundamental Christianity is to call America back to its roots, so to speak.

There is no one defining influence in fundamentalism. In its early stages, the group drew from many different denominations and traditions—Reformed, Revivalistic, etc. However, in recent years the movement has largely been associated with a strange mix of Keswick/Revivalism theology. The believer is seen to have two natures—one fleshly (sinful) and the other spiritual. As with Keswick spirituality, most fundamentalists believe that the Christian is to fight this sinful nature by calling on the power of the Holy Spirit. Yet unlike Keswick, there is no final victory over the flesh. There is a constant struggle in this life between the evil desires of the flesh and the good desires of the spirit.

In fundamentalism, spirituality is largely defined on a behavioral basis. This is seen as a direct result of the movement placing such great emphasis for so many years on the outward, verifiable tests for truth and obedience. Edward J. Carnell maintained that, " … fundamentalism was orthodoxy gone cultic because its convictions were not linked with the historic creeds of the Church and it was more of a mentality than a movement." Similarly, Carl F. H. Henry charged that "fundamentalists did not present Christianity as an overarching world view but concentrated instead on only part of the message. They were too other-worldly, anti-intellectual, and unwilling to bring their faith to bear upon culture and social life" (both quotes cited by Pierard).

This shift toward an *non-historical devotional piety* as well as *a general retreat from culture and society* became the defining influences in fundamentalist spirituality. Houghton suggests that the marks of true spirituality in the more extreme factions of this movement include:

1. **Legalism**: Exhibits an extremely negative attitude toward everything in the world (music, movies, novels, parties). *Second-step separation* is practiced (don't buy groceries from a store that sells alcohol).

2. **Tithing**: Guilt is imposed as a motivator if giving to church drops below 10% of income.

3. **Revivalism**: Evangelistic meetings are held twice a year to win the lost and stir Christians to rededicate their lives.

4. **Soul-Winning**: This criteria is probably the greatest evidence of one's spirituality. Training courses are given to teach people how to win the lost-soul to Christ. A very confrontational style is usually advocated.

5. **Dogmatism**: Narrow views are strongly defended. Fellowship with others is based on believing and saying the same thing.

6. **Activism**: Involvement in all the church programs is near mandatory.

7. **Anti-Intellectualism**: Scholarship that is outside of their own circle is distrusted and attacked. An example of this is the "King-James Only" movement.

8. **Cultural Barrenness**: A Rapture mentality prevents them from participating in or appreciating the arts.

9. **Missions**: Guilt is imposed as a motivator again if the believer does not take part in missions or give direct support to a missionary.

Although this list sounds very negative (and it is) it must be remembered that this is largely what Fundamentalism *has become*. Few sympathetic to conservative Christianity would deny that the original goals of the movement were noble. At the same time, however, they were somewhat naïve. Trying to avoid the risk of becoming too "cultural" and thereby compromising Christian truth, the fundamentalists (in purest form) became too dogmatic and compromised their *credibility* in modern culture (both secular and Christian).

The major lesson to be learned from the fundamentalist movement is that the truth *is* to be defended, but not with tactics that make it irrelevant and unattractive to those we are seeking to win to Christ. It is difficult to live out the old admonition of "being *in* the world, but not *of* the world." Paul admonishes the Ephesians to "speak the truth in love" to one another (Ephesians 4:15). In Revelation, the Lord Jesus praises the same church for standing against evil, but rebukes them for losing the love they had at first. *We should not forget that our goal is not to win the **argument**, but to win the hearts and minds of those who are opposed to Christ.*

Evangelicalism

"Evangelical" is a term that has been used since the time of The Reformation when it was attached to Lutherans who sought to redirect Christianity to the renewing authority of God's Written Word and to recover the power of the True Gospel. The *evangelical spirit* has manifest itself throughout the history of the Church in the people and movements who have called the Christian community back to pure *proclamation* and *incarnation* of the Gospel—the good news *of* Christ *about* Christ. It's roots are laid in the early Apostolic church and its branches re-surge in the works of people like Peter Waldo, John Wycliffe, Nicolaus Zinzendorf, John Wesley, Billy Graham, John Stott, John Piper... and the list goes on.

Theologically Evangelicalism has been characterized by an emphasis on the sovereignty and holiness of God, the total depravity and sinfulness of humanity, the inspiration and inerrancy of the Bible, the substitutionary atonement of Christ, salvation by God's unmerited grace in Christ, and the preaching of the Gospel as a means to reform people, society and culture in general. Today the term "evangelical" is applied across a great diversity of peoples and denominations. The *Evangelical movement* has generally united theologically divergent groups by the call to a simple expression of the fundamentals of Christianity.

Evangelicalism as we know it today developed out of the Fundamentalist movement of the early half of the 20th Century as Christianity was engaged in the battle with the secular humanist forces for the right to be *THE* religion of America. The urban revivalist efforts of men like Charles Finney and D. L. Moody in the 1800's laid the foundation for this movement. The work being done on the "frontier" by the Baptists, Methodists, Disciples of Christ, Presbyterians and the early Holiness movement spread the Gospel across the land and began to slowly but surely transform individuals and therefore, the culture.

Evangelicalism began essentially as a grass roots movement that took hold in the soil of both white and black communities. For the black community, the church often served as the center of cultural development both during the years of slavery and after emancipation. In white communities antislavery campaigns along with other social causes were birthed out of evangelical revivalism as it provided the vision to reform and cleanse culture and society to produce a righteous republic. Without the influence of the evangelical spirit, many of the social reforms of the late 19th and early 20th Century would have never been born.

Evangelicalism became intertwined with protestant denominations which shaped American values. By the 20th Century political leaders often held general evangelical convictions and suppressed non-protestant people and ideas which did not line up with the growing vision of America as God's chosen people and "a city set on a hill" as an example for all the world. Evangelical protestantism soon defined "civil religion" in America.

A defining force in modern evangelicalism was the break it made with Fundamentalism beginning in the early 1940s. The founding of the National Association of Evangelicals (1942), Fuller Theological Seminary (1947), and *Christianity Today* (1956) became "significant expressions" of "new" or "neo-evangelicalism." This movement criticized the older Fundamentalists for now having,

> "...a wrong attitude [a suspicion of all who did not hold every doctrine and practice that fundamentalists did], a wrong strategy [a separatism that aimed at a totally pure church on the local and denominational levels], and wrong results [it had not turned the tide of liberalism anywhere nor had it penetrated with is theology into the social problems of the day]" (Pierard).

If the major problem associated with Fundamentalism was that it distanced itself too far from culture, then the major problem with Evangelicalism is that it often embraced culture too closely. This is seen particularly in the movement's affinity with so called conservative politics and democratic capitalism in general.

The Evangelical understanding of the Church began to shift from the biblical pastoral metaphor of leadership exhibited by service and shepherding, to a metaphor based more on business practice with the pastor becoming the CEO leading a group of individuals who all carried the power to vote and thereby establish church polity.

Richard Lints has suggested three main characteristics that have come to define the Evangelical movement: 1) inductive Bible study, 2) para-church orientation, and 3) a non-historical devotional piety.

Inductive Bible Study

Pope Leo X charged that Luther's break from the Roman church would lead to 1,000 different interpretations of Christianity with a 1,000 different churches. The Pope was prophetic. The study of the Bible within Evangelicalism (as with all of Protestantism) has become *an essentially private matter.* The assumption of this method is that the biblical text is accessible to anyone who will spend a little time with it.

The danger here is *subjectivism.* "In banishing all mediators between the Bible and ourselves, we have let the Scriptures be ensnared in a web of subjectivism" (Lints 93). The *sola scriptura* of The Reformation did not mean, "Me and the Bible alone," much less, "What the Bible means to me." Instead the reformers affirmed that the text was to be interpreted in light of itself within the "communion of saints." Yet in evangelicalism's strong emphasis on the democratic ideal, each individual has just as much right to give his or her "two cents worth" as the next person, regardless of training or maturity.

Nevertheless, a division has been fostered between the "common folk" and the "academics." The theologians, centered in the major seminaries, speak a language that most people outside their circles don't understand or care about. Instead of trying to correct this problem by educating pastors to be educators of the people they serve, there has been a popular appeal to "dumb down" theology to make it easy to digest. Jonathan Edwards would often preach sermons with 30 or more "points." Today most church goers barely tolerate three. This "dumbing

146

down" goes hand in hand with a general ignorance and lack of education wrecking the West generally, and America specifically.

Since critical open debate has become increasingly intolerable, there has been a more *pluralistic* stance taken toward theology. *To claim to know the truth may offend someone else, so it is better to smile and nod your head in feigned agreement than to disagree.*

Seminaries in America used to lay a foundation of Greek and Hebrew studies upon which all other theological building was done. As more seminaries drop their original language requirements, theology becomes more of a popularity game often resulting in church leaders having a mish-mash of competing theologies. This has created much fragmentation within the major Protestant traditions. *Theology, as a serious intellectual and spiritual pursuit, is quickly disappearing within Evangelicalism.*[57]

Para-church Orientation

Much of the ministry of Evangelicalism has been centralized in *para-church* organizations. The problem here lies in the fact that a larger theological vision must be pluralized and shortened to accommodate the various 'groups' that may unite under the organizational framework.

Although many of these groups have done much good in preaching the Gospel and ministering to culture and society, they have, nevertheless, been somewhat destructive to the theological vision of the Church. Since these groups unite people from such diverse backgrounds (Reformed, Wesleyan, Pietist, Revivalist), it becomes impossible to formulate a set of doctrines to satisfy all who participate in the ministry. This in turn fosters *a lack of cohesive tradition* and a general *truncation of theology* to include only the "essentials." Yet one wonders how the rich complexity of Biblical Truth can be diluted to a set of five or six core dogmas without doing damage to the overall shape set in the Biblical narrative? *A shallow theology enriches no one.*

---

57   See David Wells *No Place of Truth* and *God in the Wasteland* for a complete development of these themes.

Non-Historical Devotional Piety

Linked to the disappearance of theology, Evangelicals have largely lost any real desire to access the great works of the Faith. What is worse, they see no real importance in this pursuit. As Richard Lints points out, Christians today look back, if they look back at all, to C. S. Lewis' publication of *Mere Christianity* in 1952 as the fountainhead of Christian spirituality (62). The modern evangelical assumes that anything of importance has happened within the last hundred years (probably more like the last 5 years!) thus missing the rich tradition from centuries past.

To make matters worse, many contemporary Christians cannot be bothered to expend any effort in critical thinking; for most this is *just too hard*. What more could one need other than a "devotion" that can be read in five minutes or less? *This is not just a spiritual or theological issue*. With the collapse of education in the West over the past 75 years, a great majority of people in America are *functionally illiterate* and have no historical perspective from which to make sense of any historical realities.[58]

As a result, theology within the Church has been replaced with a more secularized psychology that promotes well being of the self above all else. A browse through the "Best Sellers" rack at the local Christian bookstore confirms this fact. The concerns for holiness, morality, Christlikeness have been replaced by the need for healthy self-image, significance, and success.

These three factors alone have shaped Evangelicalism into a movement that is based more on its politics and social concerns rather than theology as a means to see Christ more clearly and follow Him more closely. The core tenets of orthodox spirituality and sanctification that we have discussed in the previous views have largely been assumed in Evangelicalism. *That is to say, this movement is characterized by its inclu-*

---

58 Although many people in our culture have the ability to read, often they do not practice extended reading for pleasure or instruction (a sign of true literacy). The inability to comprehend texts written outside their "comfort zone" means that many are cut off from older avenues of wisdom.

sion of people from all denominations and movements who have united not as a result of theological agreement, but on the basis of practicality and expediency. There is no one theology that best describes Evangelical spirituality. There is a continual emphasis given to the importance of the Gospel, the authority of the Scriptures, and the Return of Christ, but there remains much confusion and debate about what any of these things actually mean, much less what relevance they have for life in the here and now.

Nevertheless, the "evangelical spirit" has always been a catalyst for recovery, renewal, and new growth among Christ's people. In the first decade of the 21st Century evangelicalism has received another "restorationist" infusion of movement by a renewed call to get back to the core truths that shape and drive the Church.

Most prominent among these, are the voices calling for a return to the so called "5-Fold Ministry" set out by Paul in Ephesians 4:11-16. In this passage, Paul mentions the Apostles, Prophets, Evangelists, Shepherds and Teachers who equip the saints for the work of ministry/service for the goal of attaining "oneness" and "Christlikeness"—spiritual maturity. This emphasis often goes hand in hand with the "missional movement" which seeks to remind the Church that we are not a static institution, but a movement sent out by Christ to seek and save those who are lost.[59]

Parallel to this development is a resurgence in the emphasis on spiritual formation and discipleship through traditional practices now often forgotten by the "modern" church.[60] Some have hopes that first quarter of the 21st Century will see a New Reformation in which Ecclesiology—the doctrine of the Church—is reformed to *finish* the work that was started by The Reformers.[61]

---

59 Michael Frost and Alan Hirsch have been significant voices in this movement. See *The Shaping of Things to Come: Innovation and Mission for the 21st-Century Church* for a good introduction to some basic ideas.

60 The works of Dallas Willard, particularly *The Divine Conspiracy, The Spirit of the Disciplines,* and *Renovation of the Heart,* are exceptional works in this area.

61 Many have pointed out that although the Reformers recovered a Biblical view

CONCLUSIONS

> "Spirituality in the New Testament sense is not a moral program, not a set of rules, not a level of ethical achievement, not a philosophy, not a rhetoric, not an idea, not a strategy, not a theory of meditation, but rather simply **life lived in Christ**" (Oden *emphasis mine*).

Every Christian has already formed a view of what it means to be spiritual. Often, however, we have not thought reflectively or critically about our view particularly in light of Biblical revelation. Most often, either the strong force of *tradition* or *culture* has shaped what we believe *and we never question what he have been taught.*

When our personal views are criticized we feel threatened. Hopefully, after having read this book, you will seek further study, not only of your own view, but of others as well. The value of knowing the various approaches to the Christian life is that you begin to build an *objective* framework within which to evaluate the views that might be encountered. This in turn gives you the ability to validate your views against the Truth of Scripture, as well as validate its viability to be lived on a daily basis. We need to know *what* we believe and *why* we believe it.

The pursuit of spirituality implies the idea of *change*. Apart from change nothing is gained. At the focal point of change there is a concept more universal and transcendent than all others—*hope*. We seek to be spiritual because we think that either it will make our life better now, or hold promise for us in the world to come. For the true disciple of Christ,

---

of salvation, they kept an essentially Roman Catholic form of church practice and thus were never able affect a *complete* reform of Christianity.

the pursuit of holiness should not focus so much on the achievement of the individual, but in the satisfaction of The Teacher. We should pursue Christlikeness not merely for the benefits that it brings us, but because ultimately it brings honor to our Teacher, our Savior, our King.

The thing that we must guard against is becoming too *complacent* in our pursuit of the truth in Christ. *As we study the Bible, many of our views will (and should) change or be modified.* In a very real sense, we should continue to learn and grow until we die. We must remain flexible enough to allow new ideas (at least new from our perspective) to affect the way we think about ourselves, our relationship to God, and our place in history.

Most people are "eclectic" in their practice of spirituality. This means they often synthesize the strengths of several systems of belief into a new system, a "personal culture and tradition." One thing that must be stated clearly at the end of this study that you should already be aware of: ***There is no one system that encompasses all truth.*** Every system that we have looked at has imbalances; some contain blatant heresy. Each of these traditions was originally founded by men who had a sincere desire to know and practice the truth; however, *it is not impossible to be sincerely wrong.*

Another warning we learn from History: *A view is not right because it is successful.* Some of the most successful men in history have been heretics who taught contrary to the truth. This is a hard lesson for a modern American raised in a capitalistic, "free" republic to comprehend: *Success does not equal Truth.* All that glitters is not gold, just as everyone who has many followers is not always on the right path. In fact, Jesus himself warns us about carcasses and gathering vultures (see Matthew 24:23-28).

Wisdom teaches that we should not be too eager to change our views to the standard of *what is happening now.* Nor should we change our views because we discover an insight from a theologian who lived 1,000 years ago. Study, reflect, and analyze what you learn. Part of becoming an educated Christian means that you must grow and in order to grow you must change. *Healthy growth takes time.* We study the past so that we may know how to live in the present and what to expect in the future. And with so many competing forces pulling at us in modern (*postmodern, or post-postmodern*) culture we cannot afford to lose the insights and teaching of those who have come before us in our shared Christian tradition.

As I stated at the beginning, I believe that the final test for any system of faith and practice should contain two foundational ideas: 1) It must be in line with the Truth of Scripture, and 2) It must point clearly to Jesus Christ as Creator, Savior and King. We may always have disagreements about what Scripture *means*, but not about what it *says*.

We must also not forget that this is not just an intellectual exercise. The Father keeps company with us through the presence of His Spirit. The Spirit is here to guide us to The Truth—to Christ—and to empower us to live in The Way that is truly pleasing to The Father. Our Lord and Savior Jesus promised never to leave or forsake us. *The Three-In-One God is ever present with us to guide us home.* Part of pursuing Him is learning to hear His leading through the Scriptures of course, but also in the circumstances of life, and through the voices of other mature brothers and sisters in Christ.

Our world and our cultures are dying and passing away. We must contend with the current cultural lie that actions do not have consequences. *This could not be further from the truth.* In fact, our decisions and thoughts have consequences, not merely our actions. Our goal in pursuing spirituality is to make the most of our relationship with Father-God. We seek to please Him. We seek to know Him better. We seek to be witnesses for Him in a fallen, dying world. *Yet we must always balance our fervent desire for an experience of the Other with a strong commitment to Biblical truth.*

> "God is spirit, and those who worship Him
> must worship in spirit and truth." (The Lord Jesus, John 4:24)

BIBLIOGRAPHY

Abbreviations:

EDT: *Evangelical Dictionary of Theology*. Grand Rapids: Baker, 1984.

NDT: *New Dictionary of Theology*. Downers Grove: Intervarsity, 1988.

Albin, T. R. "Spirituality" in NDT.

Bratcher , Robert G. "The Meaning of Sarx ("Flesh") in Paul's Letters." *The Bible Translator* 29 (April 1978): 212-218.

Bray, G. L. "Eastern Orthodox Theology" in NDT.

_____. "Iconoclastic Controversies" in NDT.

_____. "Deification" in NDT.

Brown, D. W. "Pietism" in NDT.

Burge, G. M. "Sin, Mortal" in EDT.

Charley, J. W. "Roman Catholic Theology" in NDT.

Cranfield, C. E. B. "Paul's Teaching on Sanctification." *Reformed Review* 48 (Spring 1995): 217-229.

Cunliffe-Jones, Hubert, ed. *A History of Christian Doctrine*. New York: T&T Clark, 1978.

D'Sena, George W. *The Will of God, Your Sanctification*. Toronto: The Peoples Church, 1971.

Deiter, Melvin E. "Revivalism" in EDT.

_____. "The Wesleyan Perspective." *Five Views on Sanctification*. Ed. Stanley N. Gundry. Grand Rapids, MI: Academie, 1987.

Dicker, Gordon S. "Luther's Doctrines of Justification and Sanctification." *Reformed Theological Review* 26 (1967): 11-16.

Demarest, Bruce, ed. *Four Views on Christian Spirituality.* Zondervan, 2012.

Dicker, Gordon S. "Luther's Doctrines of Justification and Sanctification." *Reformed Theological Review* 26 (1967): 11-16.

_____. "Luther's Doctrines of Justification and Sanctification II." *Reformed Theological Review* 26 (1967): 65-71.

Dockery, David S. "Romans 7:14-25: Pauline Tension in the Christian Life." *Grace Theological Journal* 2 (Fall 1981): 239-257.

Driskill, Joseph. "The Progressive Face of Mainline Protestant Spirituality." *Four Views on Christian Spirituality.* Ed. Bruce Demarest. Grand Rapids: Zondervan, 2013.

Dunn, James D. G. "Salvation Proclaimed: VI. Romans 6:1-11." *The Expository Times* 93 (June 1982): 259-263.

Ferguson, Sinclair B. "The Reformed View." *Christian Spirituality: Five Views of Sanctification.* Ed. Donald Alexander. Downers Grove, IL: InterVarsity, 1988. 47-91.

Finney, Charles G. *Revival Lectures.* Grand Rapids, MI: Revell, 1993.

Forde, Gerald O. "The Lutheran View." *Christian Spirituality: Five Views of Sanctification.* Ed. Donald Alexander. Downers Grove, IL: InterVarsity, 1988.

Forsyth, P. T. "Christian Perfection" in *God the Holy Father,* Edinburgh: The Saint Andrews Press, 1957, pp. 97-148.

Galli, Mark, and Ted Olsen. *131 Christians Everyone Should Know.* Nashville, TN: Broadman & Holman, 2000.

González, Justo L. *The Story of Christianity: The Early Church to the Dawn of The Reformation.* Volumes 1 &2. San Francisco: Harper Collins, 1985.

Hahn, Scott. "Come to The Father: The Fact at the Foundation of Catholic Spirituality." *Four Views on Christian Spirituality.* Ed. Bruce Demarest. Grand Rapids: Zondervan, 2013. 73-94.

Hannah, John D. "The Church to the Modern Era" Unpublished class notes. Dallas Theological Seminary, Spring 1995.

_____. "The Church in the Modern Era." Unpublished class notes. Dallas Theological Seminary, Spring 1995.

Hillyer, P. N. "Mystical Theology" in NDT.

Hinson, E. Glenn. "The Contemplative View." *Christian Spirituality: Five Views of Sanctification*. Ed. Donald Alexander. Downers Grove, IL: InterVarsity, 1988. 171-200.

Hoekema, Anthony A. "The Struggle Between the Old and New Natures in the Converted Man." *Bulletin of the Evangelical Theological Society* 2 (Spring 1962): 42-50.

Houghton, Jerry. "Christian Spirituality." Unpublished class notes. Crichton College, Spring 1993.

Hope, N. V. "Campbell, Alexander" in EDT.

Horton, Stanley M. "The Pentecostal Perspective." *Five Views on Sanctification*. Ed. Stanley N. Gundry. Grand Rapids, MI: Academie, 1987.

Howard, Evan. "Evangelical Spirituality." *Four Views on Christian Spirituality*. Ed. Bruce Demarest. Grand Rapids: Zondervan, 2013.

Johnson, S. Lewis. "A Survey of the Biblical Psychology in the Epistle to the Romans." ThD. DTS: , 1949.

Karlberg, Mark W. "Israel's History Personified: Romans 7:7-13 in Relation to Paul's Teaching on the 'Old Man.'" Trinity Journal 7 NS (Spring 1986): 65-74.

Lane, A. N. S. "Mary" in NDT.

Leaver, Robin A. "The Hymn Explosion," *Christian History* 10 (1991).

Leith, John H. *Introduction to the Reformed Tradition*. Atlanta: John Knox Press, 1981.

Lesta, Ken. "The Nature of Sanctification in the New Testament," *Biblical Viewpoint* 14 (1980): 150-157.

Lints, Richard. *The Fabric of Theology*. Eerdmanns, 1993.

Lloyd-Jones, D. Martin. *Romans: An Exposition of Chapters 7:1-8:4. The Law: Its Functions and Limits*. Grand Rapids: Zondervan, 1974.

156

Lutzer, Erwin W. *The Doctrines That Divide: A Fresh Look at the Historic Doctrines That Separate Christians.* Grand Rapids, MI: Kregel Publications, 1998.

McAvoy, Steven L. "Paul's Concept of the Old Man." ThM thesis. DTS. June 1979.

McIntire, C. T. "Fundamentals, The" in EDT.

McKennit, Loreena. *The Mask and the Mirror.* CD. Warner Brothers, 1994.

McQuilkin, J. Robertson. "The Keswick Perspective." *Five Views on Sanctification.* Ed. Stanley N. Gundry. Grand Rapids, MI: Academie, 1987.

Milne, D. J. W. . "Romans 7:7-12. Paul's Pre-Conversion Experience." *The Reformed Theological Review* 43 (January-April 1984): 9-17.

Moo, D. J. "Israel and Paul in Romans 7:7-12." *New Testament Studies* 32 (January 1986): 122-35.

Morris, Leon. *The Cross in the New Testament.* Grand Rapids: Eerdmans, 1965.

Murray, John. "Definitive Sanctification." *Calvin Theological Journal* 2 (1967): 5-21.

Nassif, Bradley. "Orthodox Spirituality: A Quest for Transfigured Humanity." *Four Views on Christian Spirituality.* Ed. Bruce Demarest. Grand Rapids: Zondervan, 2013.

Noll, Mark A. *A History of Christianity in the United States and Canada.* Grand Rapids: Eerdmans, 1992.

_____. "Pietism" in EDT.

_____. *Turning Points: Decisive Moments in the History of Christianity.* Grand Rapids, MI: Baker, 1997.

Oden, Thomas C. "The Death of Modernity and Postmodern Evangelical Spirituality" in *The Challenge of Postmodernism.* Wheaton:Bridgepoint, 1995.

Pierard, R. V. "Evangelicalism" in EDT.

Pollock, John. "A Hundred Years of Keswick." *Christianity Today,* 19 1975, 920-922.

Porter, S. E. "Holiness, Sanctification." *The Dictionary of Paul and His Letters*. Downers Grove: Intervarsity, 1993.

Preus , R. D. "Lutheranism and Lutheran Theology." in NDT.

Postman, Neil. "Science and the Story We Need." *First Things*. January 1997. Web.

Rennie, I. S. "Evangelical Theology" in NDT.

Scaer, David P. "Sanctification in the Lutheran Confessions." *Concordia Theological Quarterly* 53 (1989): 165-181.

Scott, F. V. "John Wimber and the Vineyard Ministries" notes referenced on www.inplainsite.org. web.

Spittler, Russell P. "The Pentecostal View." *Christian Spirituality: Five Views of Sanctificatio*n. Ed. Donald Alexander. Downers Grove, IL: InterVarsity, 1988. 133-168.

Toussaint, Stanley D. "The Contrast between the Spiritual Conflict in Romans 7 and Galatians 5." *Bibliotheca Sacra* 123 (October-December 1966): 310-314.

Towns, Elmer L. "Martin Luther on Sanctification." *Bibliotheca Sacra* 126 (1969): 115-122.

Van Rensburg, S. P. J. J. "Sanctification According to the New Testament." *Neotestamentica* 1 (July 1967): 73-87.

Wadkins, Timothy H. "Christian Holiness: Positional, Progressive, and Practical. Martin Luther's View of Sanctification." *Trinity Journal* 7 (Spring 197): 57-66.

Walvoord, John F. "The Augustinian-Dispensational Perspective." Five Views on Sanctification. Ed. Stanley N. Gundry. Grand Rapids, MI: Academie, 1987.

Wilkin, Robert N. "We Believe In: Sanctification–Part 2: Past Sanctification." *Journal of the Grace Evangelical Society* 6 (Spring 1993): 3-18.

Wimber, John. *Power Evangelism*. Chosen Books, 1986.

Wood, Lawrence W. "The Wesleyan View." *Christian Spirituality: Five Views of Sanctificatio*n. Ed. Donald Alexander. Downers Grove, IL: InterVarsity, 1988.

Wright, D. F. "Platonism" in NDT.

59585820R00096

Made in the USA
Charleston, SC
09 August 2016